INSIDE THE WIRE

INSIDE THE WIRE

A MILITARY INTELLIGENCE SOLDIER'S EYEWITNESS ACCOUNT OF LIFE AT GUANTÁNAMO

ERIK SAAR
AND VIVECA NOVAK

THE PENGUIN PRESS
NEW YORK
2005

THE PENGUIN PRESS
Published by the Penguin Group
Penguin Group (USA) Inc., 375 Hudson Street, New York, New York 10014, U.S.A. • Penguin Group
(Canada), 10 Alcorn Avenue, Toronto, Ontario, Canada M4V 3B2 (a division of Pearson Penguin
Canada Inc.) • Penguin Books Ltd, 80 Strand, London WC2R 0RL, England • Penguin Ireland,
25 St. Stephen's Green, Dublin 2, Ireland (a division of Penguin Books Ltd) • Penguin Books
Australia Ltd, 250 Camberwell Road, Camberwell, Victoria 3124, Australia (a division of Pearson
Australia Group Pty Ltd) • Penguin Books India Pvt Ltd, 11 Community Centre, Panchsheel Park,
New Delhi – 110 017, India • Penguin Group (NZ), Cnr Airborne and Rosedale Roads,
Albany, Auckland 1310, New Zealand (a division of Pearson New Zealand
Ltd) • Penguin Books (South Africa) (Pty) Ltd, 24 Sturdee Avenue,
Rosebank, Johannesburg 2196, South Africa

Penguin Books Ltd, Registered Offices:
80 Strand, London WC2R 0RL, England

First published in 2005 by The Penguin Press,
a member of Penguin Group (USA) Inc.

1   3   5   7   9   10   8   6   4   2

CIP data available.
ISBN 1-59420-066-1

This book is printed on acid-free paper. ⊛

Printed in the United States of America

Designed by Claire Vaccaro
Map by Jeffrey L. Ward

For Darcie Lynn

—E.S.

To Bob, Nora, and Thomas

—V.N.

AUTHORS' NOTE

The names of most individuals mentioned in this book have been changed to protect their privacy or because the Department of Defense considers them "for official use only." That includes the identities of detainees at Camp Delta, unless they are footnoted. My group of friends from Pennsylvania, as well as my girlfriend (now wife), have been identified by their actual first names only. The following names have not been changed because they have received extensive exposure in the press:

U.S. Army Major General Keith Alexander
Former U.S. Air Force Senior Airman Ahmad al Halabi
Ahmed Mehalba
U.S. Army Major General Geoffrey Miller
Secretary of Defense Donald Rumsfeld
Former Army Chief of Staff General Eric Shinseki

Former U.S. Army Captain James Yee

Usama bin Laden

Mohammad Atta

Hani Hanjour

Saddam Hussein

Former Secretary of State Colin Powell

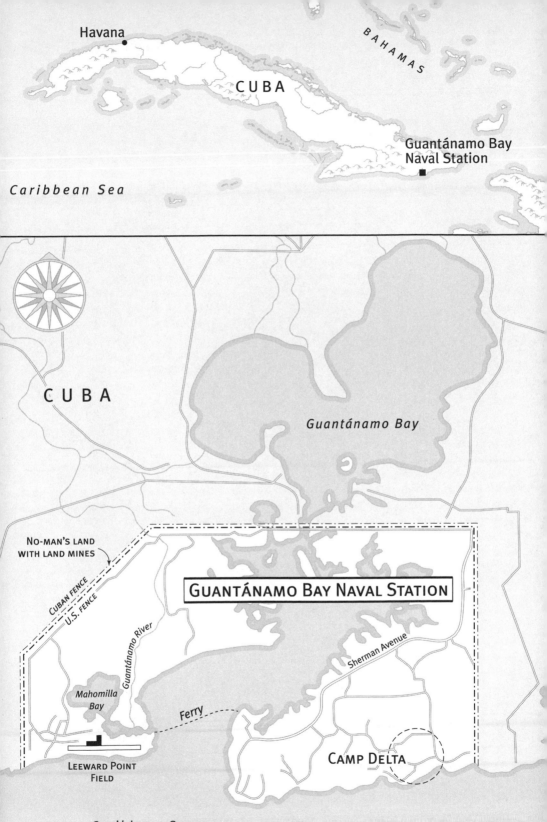

Havana

B A H A M A S

CUBA

Guantánamo Bay
Naval Station

Caribbean Sea

C U B A

Guantánamo Bay

NO-MAN'S LAND
WITH LAND MINES

CUBAN FENCE

U.S. FENCE

Guantánamo River

GUANTÁNAMO BAY NAVAL STATION

Sherman Avenue

*Mahomilla
Bay*

Ferry

LEEWARD POINT
FIELD

CAMP DELTA

Caribbean Sea

© 2005 Jeffrey L. Ward

PROLOGUE

At 0500 on 9/11, it was touch and go who would win: me or the stack of metal folding chairs I was trying to wrestle into place on the parade field at the U.S. Army Intelligence Center, Fort Huachuca, Arizona. A change-of-command ceremony was scheduled for later that morning, and prepping for it was the kind of task that fell to junior enlisted peasants like me. It wasn't yet daybreak and I was winding myself up with unspoken gripes. For this the army spent two years teaching me Arabic? To check oil in Humvees and set up chairs to celebrate some new one-star? I'd joined the army to get into military intelligence (MI) work, but I'd done damn little of that so far. If I'd lived a normal life after college instead of enlisting, would I be doing something more meaningful now?

Hell yes, I would. I'd be sleeping.

Driving back to the barracks, I heard the news of a plane hitting the World Trade Center's North Tower. Rushing to my room, I flipped on the TV and watched as the second plane sliced into the South Tower. Shit. There was no doubt this was a terrorist attack. I'd been scheduled for duty in New York starting in August, doing intel work for the FBI right near the Trade Center. I had been dying to get there, but my orders hadn't been cut on time, and I'd been stuck in Arizona. But for that, I would have been one of those stunned and terrified people watching the towers burn from their windows or the street and wondering what other hell might break loose all around them.

My thoughts flashed back to the trips our family had taken to New York at least twice a year. We'd go for Yankee games or a show, or to see the Rockefeller Center tree and be wowed by the city's holiday glitter. We lived in Clarks Summit, Pennsylvania, a town of five thousand or so right outside of Scranton, just a two-hour drive from Manhattan, and those trips were a treat, even sandwiched in the backseat between my two older sisters. When we were about half an hour away, I'd ask my dad to tell me when he could see the Twin Towers, and I'd crane forward to get that first glimpse. They seemed monstrous to my small-town eyes, but majestic. Watching the billows of jet-black smoke stream out of the towers, I couldn't see how all of those thousands of people were going to get out alive. Then the South Tower began to collapse. As that massive column collapsed into dust before my eyes, I knew we were at war.

At 0930, Arizona time, the phone rang and my platoon sergeant ordered me to report for duty. About thirty of us assembled at Riley Barracks, where Staff Sergeant Stafford warned us that Huachuca might be on the terrorists' hit list. We were to patrol the grounds of the base for the rest of the day. The FAA had shut down commercial air traffic, and our main task was to scan the Arizona skies for any incoming madness. Of course nothing happened. The stillness of that crisp day seemed so improbable given the intensity of what had just happened. I had a lot of time to stare at the mountains around Sierra Vista and think about what it now meant to be in military intelligence and to know the language of the enemy.

The buzz on base that day was that this must be the handiwork of Usama bin Laden. Everyone I knew in the intel community believed he was serious about coming after Americans, but I wouldn't have believed he could pull off something like this. We certainly knew how deep Al Qaeda's hatred of America was, though. In my training I'd had plenty of exposure to how fanatical he and his followers were, how they wanted to ignite a holy war against the "infidels of the West" who had stationed troops in the Islamic holy land. Now the hatred would be coming right back at them, with all the military might of the combined U.S. armed forces, and I was eager to be called into action. No more folding chairs. Arabic speakers were in short supply in the military, and I knew that every one of us was now going to be gainfully employed.

I wondered if Usama bin Laden understood what he'd started.

On September 14 the president stood at Ground Zero in solidarity with the city and the nation, and later pledged that we'd be waging a whole new kind of war against the terrorists. I kept hearing IC—intel community—chatter that we were about to pull out all the stops, not only in Afghanistan but around the Muslim world. As far as most of my friends in the military and I were concerned, we couldn't go after them soon enough.

On October 7 the United States launched Operation Enduring Freedom, unleashing massive bombing strikes on Taliban and Al Qaeda strongholds in Kabul, Kandahar, and Jalalabad. The Taliban was on the run. Even as we took over vast swaths of the country, though, Bin Laden was proving elusive.

By mid-October, I was in lower Manhattan with the FBI, ten blocks from Ground Zero, close enough to absorb the rancid odor of the burning debris. You could almost feel it on your skin. Some of my new coworkers were wearing hospital masks, and I was struck by the sense of mission on their faces.

For six months in New York, I translated and analyzed voice and written communications. My colleagues were trying to come to terms with the psychological shock of the attack. All of New York was grieving. One day an FBI special agent took me behind the Ground Zero barrier into the site. We hadn't gotten far before a New York City cop stopped us—he'd noticed I wasn't wearing an FBI jacket—but we got as close as I needed to be. After more than a month, the smoke was still rising. The solemn intensity of the workers, their faces smeared with soot, digging through mountains of rubble looking for any trace at all of those who'd perished, made a permanent impression on me.

In May of 2002, I transferred to the Washington area to work with the National Security Agency (NSA) at Fort Meade. It was an assignment that allowed me to see more of the big picture of the intel support for the war on terror. The personnel there, charged with protecting our country on a strategic level, were the smartest and hardest-working people I'd ever been privileged to work with, and they were clearly providing our policy makers with pertinent information on a daily basis. Although I'm restricted from describing in any detail what I saw, the sophistication of our grasp on terrorist activities all around the world was deeply impressive. At the same time, I knew it wasn't enough, or 9/11 never could have occurred.

Back in January of that year, the Bush administration had started sending terrorist suspects from Afghanistan to Guantánamo Bay. I hoped anyone even remotely affiliated with Al Qaeda would end up there. What better place to send them than Gitmo, the military's own no-man's-land. Donald Rumsfeld had announced that Guantánamo was getting "the worst of the worst," and those in the IC figured the interrogators were going to have their work cut out for them trying to get solid intel out of those hardened fanatics.

One warm July morning at Fort Meade, while my platoon was doing cooldown stretches during physical training (PT), my ears perked up when I overheard one of the other linguists in my unit say, "When I was at Gitmo . . ." We hadn't heard much at all about what was going on down in Cuba, and I hadn't previously run into anyone who'd been to the detainee camp. I wanted to hear this guy's story.

He'd spent two weeks at Camp Delta, the new facility that had been built just for the terrorists, for some assignment that he couldn't talk about, and he'd been in on some interrogations. He said that some interrogators used "intense" tactics while others were using more of a psychological approach to try to get the terrorists to trust them. The whole operation, he told me, was extremely interesting. But he couldn't say much else because we weren't in a secure environment and I didn't have the requisite "need-to-know."

The idea of going to Gitmo intrigued me. I was absorbed in my work at Fort Meade. I had a top secret security clearance, and I was learning a hell of a lot about intel gathering and analysis. I'd also started dating a woman who I was pretty sure was the real thing for me. Darcie and I had first met back in 1998 through mutual friends, at a beach party in Avalon, New Jersey. It had become an annual rite, with the same group coming together every June. I'd seen her every year there since, and I'd always been attracted to her, but she was either involved or, later, married, and so was I. When I took leave to attend the party that past June, though, things were different; both she and I were now divorced, and as fate would have it, she was in the process of moving to Washington. We started dating as soon as she got to the city. So I had good reasons to stay right where I was.

But the thought of going to Gitmo and dealing directly with the terrorists got my adrenaline going. I had wanted to get into interrogation work when I first signed up for the army: training for wartime scenarios of gathering intelligence from enemy prisoners and learning how to read people, exploit their emotions, know if you're being lied to. I thought I'd love the intellectual challenge of the mental and verbal chess match. But when I enlisted, there hadn't been any openings in the training program. Gitmo would be a great way to get some exposure to that kind of work, which I thought I might want to pursue either in the military or a civilian service.

A few weeks later, when my command asked for a linguist volunteer to do a six-month tour in Guantánamo, I raised my hand.

My family thought I was nuts when I had signed up for the army four years earlier, and my wife at the time wasn't exactly enamored of the idea either. My mom said she didn't see the logic in enlisting after getting a college degree. I'd just finished a B.S. in marketing and landed a good gig as a sales rep for United Parcel Service. But I didn't see that as a career; I was restless and impatient to do something challenging. I had been devouring books on the military and the intelligence community for a while, and the FBI and CIA attracted me. Unfortunately, those agencies had no need for a twenty-two-year-old guy with a decent curveball and a degree in marketing. But the military also had intelligence services. I'd seen some ads about the army's student loan repayment program, and since I owed the feds thirty thousand dollars, that offer was no small enticement. I also had a lot of respect for the military.

My father had been in Vietnam with the air force, a sacrifice for which his generation was anything but grateful. He never talked about it. But I'd always been proud that my dad had served. I had also been impressed when my cousin Brad, who was a decade older than me, had enlisted and served as a platoon sergeant in a tank unit that saw significant action in the Gulf War.

I'd always looked up to Brad. Sports were everything to me growing up, and Brad was the star quarterback on his high school football team. His family lived a few towns away from us, and my dad and I would go to watch his games on Friday nights. When he got back from the war, I was struck by the quiet pride with which he wore his uniform. He showed me his medals, and I gobbled up his stories about fighting the Iraqis.

At twenty-two I had never been west of the Mississippi or crossed an ocean. My wife, Debbie, and I had married young, when we were both nineteen—exactly the age at which my parents had wed—and though she'd been my high school sweetheart and we'd believed we were meant for each other, the first couple of years of our marriage had been pretty rough. Part of me thought the army might send us somewhere far away where we could work out our problems. We'd have to be apart during my basic training, but after that she'd be able to join me on most of my assignments. Debbie wasn't thrilled with the idea, but I figured this would be a defining point in our relationship: it would either grow stronger or break apart. I wasn't sure how committed she was to being together anymore, and I thought this would force a decision.

My closest friends also wondered about my sanity, but they understood it might be something I had to do. Kevin, Ryan, Timmy, Scotty, Grant, and the three Mikes—we were a close band of near brothers who had grown up together in the schools, on the sports fields, in the churches and the bars of our corner of the state. We'd been through nearly everything together: parents divorcing or passing away, basketball championships, home runs hit and surrendered, girlfriends gained and lost, countless rounds of golf.

They still called me Vern, a nickname I had acquired the summer before eighth grade at basketball camp. In those days I had a buzz cut and a talent for saying things without thinking. After witnessing a contest among the older guys to measure who could make out with a girl longest, I burst out, asking "How could you guys hold your breath that long?" One of the varsity players responded that I reminded him of Vern, the most naive of the four kids who get in over their heads in the movie *Stand by Me*. The name stuck. My boys were all pretty content with the careers they'd begun, but they understood I was in a different place, up for a little adventure.

I told the army recruiter that I wanted something that would help me get a civilian job in intelligence after one four-year hitch. Since there were no interrogation slots available, he pitched the idea of becoming a linguist, a job that came with student loan repayment, language school in Monterey, a top secret security clearance, and work in military intelligence. "If you can't get a government job after this gig, you don't deserve one," he said.

Sold. I was frankly proud of my decision, puffed up with idealism and love of country. And maybe I was a chump, or so I wondered when I started basic training at Fort Leonard Wood, Missouri. Forty-eight hours after arriving, on what's known as Zero Day, we were packed tight into cattle trucks to go to our new barracks, kernels on an ear of corn, just one of the constant reminders that individuality had no place in our new lives. The two barrel-chested, hairless drill sergeants in my truck engaged in a prolonged display of intimidation, screaming army clichés and stolen movie riffs at us: "I hope you gave your life to Jesus because your ass belongs to me!" and "There is no crying in the army!"

My undergraduate degree, of course, counted for nothing. That and the fact that I was headed for military intelligence just put me in an elite group guaranteed extra harassment by drill sergeants looking for egos to pound.

The first Friday night of basic, our platoon suffered an impromptu barracks inspection. As they say in the army, our shit was ate up. The drill sergeants, disregarding the weather, sent us outside. Roll left, roll right, push-ups, sit-ups, jogging in place, an hour-and-a-half workout in the mud with sideways rain pelting our faces. All I could think was that my boys back in Clarks Summit were a six-pack into the night already.

Over the next eight weeks, though, I learned to love the army regimen. We were taught land navigation, rifle marksmanship, first aid, and the whole bizarre code of military customs and courtesies. I liked the structure the army provided: "This is the mission." They told us what we were going to do and we did it; period. The sergeants drilled into our heads incessantly that we'd make sacrifices in the army, but it was for a higher purpose and our country might count on us some day. We were advised to memorize the values we were expected to live by—loyalty, duty, respect, selfless service, honor, integrity, personal courage—and we'd better damn well do so. In the morning we put on a uniform, and with that uniform there was the overwhelming sense that those who had worn it before us had helped secure the country for future generations.

It was grueling, absurd, and great. I came away with a new respect for the dedication and professionalism of those sergeants who had made our lives hell, and for anyone else who has served.

As great as basic was for me, it did nothing good for my faltering marriage. I found out when I got back home that while I was away, Debbie had been cheating on me. I'd been told she'd done so before, but I hadn't wanted to believe it. This time, I was done. We decided to split up, and I threw myself into the army with even more conviction.

My reward for basic training was a killer view of the Pacific from my room on the campus of what could have been a small liberal arts college in Monterey, except that everyone was in uniform. The Defense Language Institute (DLI) was paradise found—until the army told me I was scheduled to begin studying Korean.

When I'd signed up for the linguist program, I had to take the Defense Language Aptitude Battery (DLAB). Everyone who scored between 110 and the top score of 125 was supposed to take a category 4 language: Arabic, Chinese, or Korean. I'd tested into category 4, and I was hoping for Arabic. I'd been fascinated by the complexities of Middle Eastern politics and culture for years, and I'd followed the Arab-Israeli conflict especially closely. To my mind, the U.S. relationship with Israel was essential to the stability of the Middle East, and we had to do everything possible to support that nation. I was also intrigued by the tangled threads of our relationship with another key ally in the region, Saudi Arabia. Many Saudis were seething about the U.S. military presence in the kingdom, and it seemed that change had to be coming. I was hoping my language training would allow me to play some small part in our operations in the region.

So I didn't look forward to spending every other year in Korea, and the language would be practically no help when it came to finding jobs outside the army. But lightning struck. I found a soldier who was slotted to begin Arabic but had no affinity for the Middle East and loved Asian culture. She and I were given permission to swap.

Thus I was introduced to Modern Standard Arabic (MSA)—the language of the Koran and the Arabic used in most official communications and writings in the Middle East, in media broadcasts and newspapers, and in political speeches and religious discussions. I was also taught about the culture, geography, politics, and history of the Middle East by a group of six instructors—all native speakers who had emigrated to the United States from Iraq, Saudi Arabia, Lebanon, and Egypt, some of whom had fled persecution. One Iraqi instructor, Mr. Walid, came to the United States in the midnineties, after his family had been awakened one frightening night by a knock on the door. The Mukhabarat—the Iraqi Intelligence Service—were outside and its agents wanted words with Mr. Walid, who was a schoolteacher. He was taken to a dark room to be questioned. Apparently, one of the children in his class had reported to his father, who was a secret intelligence officer, that the teacher had said something controversial that day. Mr. Walid had no idea what it could have been, but throughout the night he was questioned and made to pledge his loyalty to Saddam. He believed he was going to die. After they let him go, he made plans to leave for the United States with his family as soon as possible.

The instructors at DLI became friends and mentors, and in

some ways I learned more about Middle Eastern culture from their hospitality than from my studies. My Lebanese instructor, Mr. Fareed, occasionally invited me to dinner at his home; those meals with his family were among the best learning experiences I had. During our dinners I saw enormous depth of love between the parents and their children. I also experienced the famous Arab love of conversation. Occasionally Mr. Fareed would invite Arab friends of his, and we would talk well into the night.

I was especially struck by the sincere spirit of generosity in the Arabic culture they introduced me to. Shortly after I arrived at DLI, for instance, I heard a story about a student who had told one of his instructors that he admired his watch. The instructor took it off and gave it to him, refusing to take no for an answer.

The ironies of the region were mind-blowing. Even as the Muslim countries were bound by their devotion to Islam, they were driven by bitter divisions between Sunnis and Shiites, between tribal groups of ancient origin, and between Islamic fundamentalists like the Wahhabites as well as followers of the more moderate clerics. There were further tensions between Muslims and Middle Eastern Christians. My instructors put a human face on those complexities, and I learned the value of personal experience in understanding the Muslim world.

As much as I loved DLI, it wasn't by choice that I spent nearly two years there, longer than the usual fifteen-month stay. Learning MSA proved to be a real challenge for me. When I had told my parents about my decision to become an army linguist, my mom reminded me of a note sent home in eighth grade, the year that we were all required to take a smorgasbord of foreign languages in order to decide which one we'd study in high school. I tried Latin, French, Spanish, German, and Russian. At the end of the year, the language program coordinator wrote my parents: "Your son has no aptitude for learning a foreign language and should not pursue further study."

Some students who floundered at DLI were sent to other jobs in the army; some were reassigned to easier languages. Another option was to be "rolled," to go back and study with a group that had recently begun. I was rolled, which to be honest wasn't the worst thing that could have happened to me. There was no better place than DLI for me to get over the pain of the breakup of my marriage. The student body was a collection of bright young people from all branches of military service, with a better than normal representation of women, and I adapted pretty well to being a bachelor again.

Our language study went from 0700 till 1600, then we went out for PT. On Fridays that meant a four-mile run on the beach. We studied hard and played hard, which had led someone long ago to christen DLI the Drunken Lust Institute.

My pals and I closed out the night plenty of times at the American Legion hall, which had cheap beer and a DJ. As the lights came on at 0200, the volume would go up on Lee Greenwood's "God Bless the USA." Drunken soldiers, sailors, airmen, and marines—onetime high school valedictorians, former drug addicts, daughters of wealthy parents, kids who had gone to bed hungry too often, sons following in their fa-

thers' footsteps, most of us uncertain where we'd be in a year—
we all loved every flag-waving word of that anthem.

The army had become my new life. Uncle Sam had given
me two phenomenal years along the California coast and
helped me recover from my failed marriage. I felt I had a new
purpose, and I was anxious to get into the intel part of my
training.

For that, my next orders took me to Goodfellow Air Force
Base in San Angelo, Texas, to learn more about the technical
aspects of signals intelligence, the mechanics of intercepting
communications, and the classification system used for sensitive information—the nitty-gritty of how to get and keep the
other side's secrets. Then it was to Huachuca, in the Arizona
desert, my permanent base for the next phase of the program.
At first I was disappointed. Rather than doing interesting intelligence work, I found myself giving technical briefings on
tactical MI electronic intercept and jamming equipment to
American and foreign military officers who were at the base
to take classes. Not exactly the kind of assignment I'd been
angling for. But luckily, four months after I got there an opportunity for a special training assignment came up, a one-
month Arabic immersion program in Cairo—my first
overseas trip. It also turned out to be an immersion program
in Islamic extremism.

The military had contracts with several schools in Cairo,
but the one I was assigned to, House of the Dawn, was radi-
cally Islamic, a fact that I'm sure had escaped the army. One of
the school administrators asked on the first day if any of us
were Jewish, and when we told him we weren't, he muttered

"That's good" under his breath. The women in our group were segregated from the male students. And our instructor repeatedly referred to Hamas and Hezbollah as freedom fighters.

During discussion in class one day we all countered that Hamas and Hezbollah are not freedom fighters; they are terrorists because they target civilians. He refused to yield ground, saying his belief was consistent with his religion— we were obviously blinded by the biased, "Zionist-controlled American media." As Arabic linguists we certainly knew that some in the Arab world felt that way, but hearing it firsthand was still an eye-opener.

Having grown up in a church-going family, attending services every Sunday of my life no matter what, I knew very well what it was to hold committed and passionate beliefs. For that reason, I also knew, maybe better than some of my classmates, how impossible it is to bring someone around to a different view through dialogue when their belief is associated with their faith. It just doesn't happen.

Cairo was an amazing, complicated city, in some ways deeply Islamic, but in others modern and Western. It's home to Al-Azhar University, the Middle East's center of Islamic higher education, and the minarets of strikingly beautiful mosques rise everywhere throughout the city. In addition, five times a day, every day, you hear the rhythmic call to prayer, wherever you may be.

We also saw the other side of life in Cairo, though, at the local coffee shop, where my classmates and I spent much of our free time. Cairo's coffee shops are the center of the city's social life. We frequented one that often played Western music. It was a hip and hypnotic blend of smoking den, disco, Internet café, and pool hall—a highlight of the trip. There we could mingle with the friendly, music-loving, Internet-savvy culture of Egyptian youth. I gave one young worker there a Dave Matthews Band CD, and when he played it through the shop's sound system, it was an instant hit. Political conversations were hard to avoid, but the views of the younger Arabs were a strange mix of aggravation with American policies and an obvious love of our culture.

"Why does America always support Israel?" I was often asked. One day a young man who couldn't have been more than sixteen walked into the coffee shop wearing a T-shirt that read in Arabic "Jihad, the only language Israel will understand." No question where the Egyptian youth fell on the Israel-Palestinian conflict. But they were also perfectly willing to voice their irritation with the radical brand of Islam we were being steeped in at the House of the Dawn. When I told one Egyptian twentysomething where I was taking classes, he said, "If those types of Muslims ever take over this country, we'll go back to the Dark Ages."

My time in Cairo taught me that in the Middle East, for some people, the Crusades might have happened a short ten years ago. The Islamic radicals wanted to see the conflict with Israel and the West as a religious war. In its reaction to 9/11, I hoped the United States wouldn't give them any fodder. We couldn't let them turn the war on terror into a clash of civilizations. The country was galvanized to go after the terrorists, and my hope was that we would stick to fighting the extremists and wouldn't let the struggle become a war on Islam. It was the bad seeds intent on waging jihad that we had to focus on. If my language training could possibly help in some small way to flush out the terrorists who wanted to bring on a holy war, I couldn't imagine anything more satisfying after the lengthy training I'd just gone through.

My old buddies had become more successful in conventional terms during my years in the army: there were two engineers, a rocket scientist (literally), a newspaper writer, an educator, and three businessmen. I wished I made more money and had control of my own life. But in some ways, I believed, these brothers of mine envied what I had: the ability to put on that uniform and work for more than a paycheck. My solace was that as they were living out the American dream, I was helping protect it.

I left for Gitmo on December 9, 2002.

JDOG

JOINT DETAINEE OPERATIONS GROUP

CHAPTER ONE

My girlfriend Darcie and I spent my last night in Washington sleepless and teary. We'd been together for six months and things were going remarkably well, but she still didn't understand why I had volunteered for this duty. When I had broken the news to her back in late September over dinner at our favorite Mexican restaurant, it put quite a damper on the evening. But when is the right time to tell your significant other you're leaving for six months?

"Dar, I'm going to be going away for a few months starting sometime in December," I'd blurted out as she dipped a tortilla chip in salsa.

She looked up, surprised, and said, "Where . . . why?"

When I told her I'd volunteered to go to Guantánamo Bay, she looked partly puzzled and partly pissed.

"Well, I figured this would be good for my career," I said, "and I think it will be the last time I have to go away while I'm in the army. Besides, I think it might be a good test for us."

Fumble.

"Why would you say that?" she asked me with a definite edge in her voice.

How to get out of this one? I had never loved anyone as much, never known anyone with such a passion for life, such energy. Still, I was a little freaked out about how fast I had fallen for her. She was coming off a divorce too, and I didn't want her to one day decide we were too serious. I figured that if this was the real thing, we'd be able to handle six months apart; it might even strengthen the bond. We talked the rest of the night.

Now that the day had come, I dreaded leaving her. She promised she'd wait for me. I hoped that was true.

At 600 we marched through our morning routine: Darcie showered while I made coffee and watched the news, and then I took my turn in the shower. Dar taught third grade in Fairfax County, out in Virginia, and she left for work early every day.

By the time I walked her out to her car, tears were threatening her vision again. Mine came later as I drove up the Baltimore–Washington Parkway to my condo to finish packing. I was afraid she might find life easier without me. I wanted Dar to go on living her life while I was away, but not effortlessly. What if she liked being single again?

My first flight took me to Norfolk, where I checked into the Navy Lodge, your basic Best Western-style box, for an overnight layover. I clicked through the TV stations, starting to wonder how I'd react to seeing terrorists in chains. The photos on the news of the first detainees arriving in Cuba, kneeling in the dirt and gravel in their orange suits, chains, and blackout goggles, hadn't bothered me as they had some people. I was just glad they'd been caught. Word in army circles was that some of the detainees were talking, but many were claiming not to know much. I was looking forward to finding out for myself, and hoping to get my feet wet quickly.

Camp Delta was being called a "legal black hole" by some critics. The Bush administration had designated the detainees as enemy combatants and had decided the suspects were not entitled to legal representation. Human rights activists were denouncing the camp as inhumane. Most in the intel community, including me, saw things differently. There were other things to worry about in our country as 2002 came to a close. We had still not found Usama, we were helping to shape a brand-new Afghani government, and President Bush had wanted the UN to make final demands for Saddam Hussein's unconditional compliance with weapons inspectors. War in Iraq seemed inevitable.

With military efficiency, I ordered a wake-up call in Norfolk for 0345. I didn't have to be at the airport till 0500 and it was just a fifteen-minute ride away, but I didn't want any glitches in the program. Rain was coming down in a cold, heavy curtain, so I was hardly delighted when the cabbie told me that for security reasons the lane closest to the terminal was off limits and I'd have a short walk before I got to cover. Short walk: a quarter mile in the pounding rain with 150 pounds of luggage at 0430. Maybe this inauspicious start should have told me something.

I checked six months' worth of bags, grabbed a cup of coffee at the snack shop, and settled in with *USA Today* next to a window to kill the hour before boarding. The first story that caught my eye was about preparations to send more troops to Kuwait to build up for the likely invasion of Iraq, and I wondered if my brother-in-law, a chaplain in the marines, would have to go.

Many in the IC believed overthrowing Saddam was fine, but there was a deeper, better motive for going into Iraq than the alleged WMDs. United States policy makers were well aware of the increasing hostility toward the American military in Saudi Arabia. It wasn't helping the royal House of Saud. Some, or perhaps most, of our troops would be pulling out of there, so the United States needed a footprint elsewhere in the region.

Although many of my colleagues in intel hoped that Iraqi troops would throw down their weapons and welcome us with open arms, as promised by Vice President Cheney, even the bulk of the GIs I knew wondered what would be the endgame. Who, we wondered, would be the magician to pull off the unification of Shiites, Kurds, Chaldean Christians, and Sunnis under the umbrella of democracy? Even if democracy succeeded, it might be in the form of a Shiite government that would become a close ally to theocratic Iran.

We were all unhappy about the continued ability of Usama bin Laden to evade capture. The president had lately been downplaying the importance of getting him, but everyone I knew in intel circles thought it should be on the top of our to-do list. Some of us believed he was receiving help from Pakistanis sympathetic to the cause, while others thought we simply needed more foot soldiers on the case. The problem had only been exacerbated by the shift of special operations forces from the mountains of Afghanistan to the oil fields of Iraq in preparation for invasion.

My transportation to Cuba was a regular Continental flight except that all sixty or so of us were either with the military or family members of troops. We made a pit stop in Jacksonville, then on to Guantánamo. Because we couldn't fly over the island, we had to go around it and come up from the south to the base. As we began our descent, I was glad I had a window seat as I twisted around to get as full a view as possible. I'd never been to the Caribbean, and I was amazed at the clear blue of the water. The beachfront was much rockier than I'd expected, with no vast stretches of silky smooth sand that I could see.

The airport runway came into view, with camouflaged military vehicles scattered around the grounds. There was no sign of the fencing and cell blocks of the camp. You'd never have known that one of the world's most formidable military installations lay just below. The base was spread over both sides of the mouth of Guantánamo Bay; the airport was on the leeward side, but I'd been told most of the action was over on the windward side.

Guantánamo wasn't supposed to be that bad a posting—just a little too confined. I knew there would be a decent NEX, the military version of Wal-Mart, and a few fast-food places. I'd also heard there were plenty of pools for beating the heat on days off duty. The navy called Gitmo the least worst place.

Of course, now that the other services—mostly the army—had rolled into town to help run the terrorist operation under what was being called Joint Task Force-Guantánamo, I would be surprised if the navy people still felt that way. The base had gone from barely having enough personnel to keep the lights on to being nearly as busy as it had been during the height of the cold war.

We taxied up to the airport and a group of MPs came to meet us. As I stepped out the door, I was hit by a wave of searing hot air—a shock after the cool December weather of Washington. By the time I'd taken the last step down to the broiling tarmac, a drop of sweat had already run down one cheek. Clever of me to put on a long-sleeved shirt that morning. It had to be at least 95 degrees, and the air was thick and heavy.

As the MPs approached, I found myself inspecting their haircuts—short enough to be regulation; their uniforms—not neatly pressed but not a wrinkled mess either; their boots—those of the specialist E-4, one rung below me, had a high shine, but those of the private first class E-3 hadn't seen Kiwi in weeks. An MP with a loaded M16 slung around his shoulder directed us to leave our bags on the ground and head to a waiting area about a hundred yards away. Our IDs were checked and an MP with a clipboard made sure no unexpected guests had arrived. Another, accompanied by a canine colleague, inspected our bags, making sure we had brought nothing explosive.

We spent an hour testing our deodorant in the sun, sitting around a hodgepodge of picnic tables waiting for the bus that would take us down to the ferry landing, where we'd catch a ride across to the windward side. I'd been told the leeward side had a foliage area that was occasionally used for training. My guess was that it was the navy's oasis away from us army types. From what I could see of this side, there would be no other reason to spend time here.

I started quizzing a young army specialist, who said he was coming back from a leave, about life at Gitmo.

"Do you drink?" he asked. I told him I did.

"Good. If you'd said no," he said, "I would've told you, 'You will now,' because there's not much else going on here. What people do is work and get drunk."

Though I was to end up finding a few other amusements during my stay, I'd soon learn that a good deal of beer was consumed most nights during long grousing sessions in the housing area.

The sun was blazing and the water glistened. There was an odd disconnect between the natural beauty of the place and everyone wearing their military camouflage. The island and sea were so beautiful you'd have thought you'd just arrived at a tropical vacation retreat. Yet this was where the United States had locked up some of the world's most dangerous terrorists. Welcome to Gitmo.

The base was surely a world all its own—the oldest overseas American military installation, and the only one on Communist soil. The United States first leased the forty-five acres the base covers, in the southeastern corner of Cuba, as a ship refueling station in 1903. In 1944 the lease was revised to say that the arrangement could be terminated only with the consent of both parties, or if the United States abandons it. Castro's coup in 1959 set the United States on edge, but the lease held. During the 1962 Cuban missile crisis, both sides of the seventeen-mile fence line that walls off Gitmo from its host were planted with land mines, and soldiers from each nation still watch each other through high-powered binoculars from guard towers. The United States pays Castro about four thousand dollars a year in rent, but he never cashes the checks.

A massive industrial-gray ferry took us from leeward to windward. In that oppressive heat the breeze was as sweet as landing a hot kiss midway through a first date. When we docked, I was shuffled over to a van with about twenty other personnel reporting for first duty, and we were driven to an airplane hangar for orientation.

We crowded into a makeshift classroom where various officers regaled us with two hours of briefings about security—a laundry list of dos and don'ts—and all the base-specific info that fell under the heading MWR (morale, welfare, and recreation). The good news was that it sounded like the base did have a few diversions. Some spots of coast actually had some beach, and there was outstanding snorkeling and scuba diving. Still, the only departures allowed during your stay were for emergencies, and one short leave given to each soldier. Although the fence line wasn't far from any given point on the base, no one was ever permitted to head into Cuba proper. I was to find that the island had a way of shrinking the longer you stayed there, and that two-week leave was universally viewed as a respite from which it was tough to return.

A top security official on the base laid down the law that we were not to write or talk about various aspects of the camp and its operations to anyone, or take any pictures of certain parts and features of the base. You couldn't, for example, photograph the beach if the shot included any part of the coastline near the detention camp. I was used to being tight-lipped about my work, so nothing he said unsettled me, nor did the form we had to sign at the end, which barred us from disclosing classified information.

During one of the breaks in the briefing I heard a guy in the back of the room mention that he was an Arabic linguist. I turned and realized I'd seen him around DLI, another MI linguist, but I didn't know his name. I assumed we'd be working together, so I headed back to introduce myself. He must have recognized me too, because when he saw me coming, he beat me to the intro.

Mark Rivers was a gregarious guy, bursting with energy—almost a little too much for my blood on first impression. He looked like an Irish import, about five foot ten with reddish-blond hair, bright blue eyes, and a ready smile, and so slim I figured he weighed no more than a buck fifty soaking wet.

The community of military linguists isn't large, so we soon figured out our mutual acquaintances and caught up on them. Turned out he had worked in England with a girl I'd dated briefly, before I met Darcie, who'd been more than a little unhappy with me when I broke things off. She'd decided she wasn't going to return some of my things, including a cherished Dallas Cowboys blanket, and had burned them in a little bonfire outside my barracks one night. Mark had heard the story, but he didn't seem inclined to hold it against me. He told me he'd been working with some high-tech tracking equipment in the UK, going after Al Qaeda in Afghanistan.

We were both nervous about which linguist group we'd be assigned to. When I'd first heard about the job at Gitmo, I'd assumed that all of us would be involved in the interrogations. Then I learned that there were actually two separate linguist teams working in the camp: one for interrogations and intel analysis that was part of the Joint Intelligence Group, or JIG, and one for translating day-to-day communications with the detainees, a unit of the Joint Detainee Operations Group, or JDOG (J-dog). I'd volunteered specifically because I wanted to be involved in interrogations, but there was no bagging out once you'd put your name in. It was hit or miss as to which team you'd be assigned to, even if you had intel training, because it was entirely dependent on which team was most in need of a linguist the day you arrived.

When the briefing was over, a handsome six-foot Arab American air force captain approached Mark and me, stuck out his hand, and asked, "So who is Mark and who is Erik?" Turned out we'd be in the same unit. The ease of his approach—the use of our first names, the general friendliness—wasn't the army way, but then the air force was less rigorous about military formalities.

He introduced himself as Captain Salim Mansur, our new commanding officer. He was a Sudanese-born graduate of MIT, an aerospace engineer, and a practicing Muslim—one of the Arab Americans from all the services who had been asked to volunteer for duty at the camp because the military had so few Arabic speakers.

Captain Mansur said he'd show us around the base and then take us to our housing unit. As we headed to his van, Mark immediately popped the question on both our minds. "Sir, which team of linguists are we going to be joining?"

"You'll be on the JDOG team," Captain Mansur said. Detainee Operations. Damn.

We went silent, which no doubt conveyed our disappointment. For this I'd given up working with the NSA and left Darcie free at home to meet some new guy who might come along? I figured I'd have to see if there was any way I could work out a transfer.

As I hopped into the front seat of the van and Mark climbed into the back, Captain Mansur tried to lighten the mood. "Don't worry," he said, "I think you'll both be very happy with your new team. We have a great group of people who work well together. You'll have a great six months." We could tell he wasn't giving us the full story.

He drove us down the main drag, Sherman Avenue, past the NEX, a McDonald's, a Subway, and a KFC. There was also a small video store, a credit union, a bowling alley, a dive shop, and an outdoor movie theater with bleacher seating, like an aging high school football stadium. Off the main road and up a hill were the various housing areas, which were a whole lot better than I'd been expecting. Camp Delta, Captain Mansur told us, was down the road a bit, off on its own.

As we headed to the housing complex, we drove past a moonscape that resembled a golf course only in its dreams, a couple of gyms, and two pools. A place called the Tiki Bar was an outdoor setup on a concrete slab with white plastic tables and chairs. It was set back from the water about a quarter mile but seemed to have a decent view of the bay. The other main bar was the Windjammer; a sign said that Thursday was karaoke night.

Mark and I had both figured we'd be in barracks housing, with maybe eight beds in an open bay, but here we were pulling up to a group of small stucco houses. When Captain Mansur dropped us off at our neighborhood housing office, where we were to pick up our keys and linens, he invited us to a cookout for the JDOG linguists. It was starting at around 1900 just a few houses down from ours, where some of our teammates lived. By now it was past 1700 and I was glad to hear we'd be eating soon.

Our house was meant for eight occupants, but with the addition of Mark and me, it now had nine. Still, we were thrilled with our new digs, even if the MP in the living room, the only one of our new roommates who was home, looked like he'd just been given latrine duty when he saw us. Staff Sergeant Frank Patterson was about five foot eleven, with a shaved head and a worn look. You could tell he made his living telling others what to do; he had the swollen gut to show that PT wasn't his top priority.

We had a kitchen, two and a half bathrooms, and a laundry room, but the highlight was cable TV with HBO. Sergeant Patterson told us to find open beds. We each found a room with a bed free and did some unpacking, then headed down the street to 19A for the barbecue. Christmas lights were strung loosely along the roof; it was the only house in the neighborhood acknowledging the coming holidays. Lawn chairs and cigarette butts were scattered around the carport and banana rats darted around the edges of the yard.

It wasn't a full day in Gitmo if you didn't see a banana rat, more likely a platoon of them. Take a rat, make it uglier and more possumlike, and there you have the unofficial mascot of Guantánamo Bay. They feared almost nothing and were so numerous that their droppings had to be the principal component of Gitmo soil.

About a dozen guys were hanging out, most of them clearly of Arab descent and all somewhere in their twenties. We spotted Captain Mansur at the grill, watching over the kebabs—always kebabs at that house, I was to find, never burgers and dogs—and he introduced us to the group. A short, pudgy, dark-haired guy who bore a striking resemblance to Jim Belushi came over, dug a couple of Miller Lites out of the cooler for us, and introduced himself as Turk. He was Turkish, most recently from Michigan, and had been working as an army mechanic based in Germany. There were probably even fewer fluent Turkish speakers than Arabic ones in the military, which is how he'd ended up at Camp Delta. I was intrigued because I hadn't been aware that any Turks were being held at the camp.

When Mark asked him what it was like working in the linguist group, Turk made no attempt to dress things up.

"This team has Christians, Jews, atheists, Muslims, and really conservative Muslims," he said. "All have their own opinions of this place. We spend a lot of our time together and usually end up arguing about the camp or religion—sometimes both. We have a lot of good people, but as a team we're really fucked up."

Mark and I drank our beers and listened intently. This was not your normal army get-acquainted chatter.

"Between you and me, the camp is a disaster," he continued. "Every pissant agency under the sun has sent someone here to interview the detainees, and they all fight about who gets to talk to the guy first. Then they realize he doesn't know shit."

This soldier knew nothing about us but felt free to openly criticize his unit and the mission on first meeting. Very unmilitary. I caught Mark's eye and he seemed amused.

"Most of your intel-type comrades think the two-star infantry officer at the top is about as smart as that banana rat," Turk continued. He was referring to Major General Geoffrey Miller, the commander of all detainee operations on base.

"But then I'm going by what your people say. I'm just here to drink some beer, get out on a boat when I can, and head back to Germany."

An awkward silence set in as Turk took a long pull on his beer and swallowed. Then he raised his bottle to clink with ours, said "Welcome to Gitmo," and walked away.

I could tell Mark was about to burst out laughing.

As Turk left us, someone named Khalid came over, a muscle-bound air force airplane mechanic who obviously spent most of his free time in the weight room. He was known as Rambo. We exchanged the usual pleasantries—he had come from Scott Air Force Base in Illinois, had family in Chicago, and was an Iraqi Christian who'd emigrated to the United States after the first Gulf War. In fact, he'd gained U.S. citizenship as a reward for the help he'd given American forces during the hostilities. His English was close to perfect.

After what Turk had said, I couldn't wait to ask him: "What do you think of this place?"

He didn't bite.

"People have a lot of very strong opinions about it," he said. "I'm not a very political guy. I'll let you two form your own views. Me, I'm halfway through a ninety-day assignment and hoping I go to Iraq when I'm done."

"If either of you ever needs a lifting partner, just let me know," he said as he walked away. "It's great to have you here."

Then Captain Mansur came over to introduce us to Ahmad al Halabi, who he said was perhaps the best linguist in the group. The captain pointed out that Ahmad could be extremely helpful to us, especially with some of the strong dialects we'd be hearing.

"Tasharrafna," Ahmad said. An honor to meet you. We replied in kind.

Ahmad looked to be in his midtwenties. Born in Syria, he and his family had moved to Dearborn, Michigan, when he was a teenager. He was so light skinned you'd never know he was an Arab. An air force supply clerk, Ahmad was asked to volunteer for Gitmo service, like Turk and Rambo, purely for his language skills. He'd been at the camp for about a month.

"How comfortable are you with your Arabic?" he asked.

"So-so," I answered. "I'm hoping it quickly improves a lot."

My recent work in intel had involved reading and listening, but not conversing. Mark was a little more confident in his reply.

Ahmad spoke in flawless MSA. He was warm and open; we liked him immediately.

Ahmad said we should speak from then on only in Arabic, but within a few minutes we had reverted to English. Mark asked our new favorite question: what Ahmad thought of the camp after his first month there.

"I'm not going to influence you two with how I feel about it," he said. "You can decide for yourselves starting tomorrow. There are some really great people on our team and we're glad you guys are here."

With that he said he was heading home.

"Massalama," I said to him. With peace.

Mark and I called it a night around 2030. As we said our good-byes, our teammates told us to be back there by 0645 for the ride to Camp Delta.

As soon as we were out of hearing, Mark said, "Well, that was odd."

"Yeah, really," I said. "I just have to wonder if these people actually get along."

"Are you nuts?" Mark said. "There is no way that group gets along. You did study Arabic, right? Erik, after fifty years the Arab world can't even get along well enough to get rid of Israel, whom they all hate! How do you think they are going to get along in a place like this?"

All I knew was that we were going to be in close quarters with these people for the next half a year, and the group dynamics seemed terrible. We were about to find they weren't going to be any better back at our new home.

When we walked through the door, we met the rest of our new housemates, who were scattered around the living room watching TV. Mark and I, two military intelligence guys, had somehow been assigned to live with seven MPs. They openly shared their pure delight with this scenario.

Sergeant Brian McNeil, a tough-looking, wiry white guy, wore a military high and tight haircut and seemed especially pleased to see us. As soon as we walked through the door, he said, "Patterson told us you guys are MI; we moved your shit. You have your own room now."

"Um . . . all right." I stuttered. We hadn't even met this asshole yet.

Sitting on the best chair the house had to offer, a powder-blue recliner whose wooden handle was prone to falling off, was Sergeant Jim Wilkinson. As soon as McNeil finished, Wilkinson chimed in without taking his eyes off the TV. "Don't eat anything that isn't yours, and touch my beer and I'll fuckin' kill you!"

Wonderful. Intros no longer necessary, we were now as close as brothers. I started to head upstairs to put my stuff away, but Mark hung back and tried to engage them in conversation. He managed to get out of them that three were part of a canine unit at the camp, including Wilkinson, who led the canine group.

"So what do you guys do with the dogs here?" Mark asked.

"We can't tell you that," Wilkinson replied flatly, continuing to stare at the TV.

"Sure you can," said Mark, being a smartass. "I'm in intelligence."

Wilkinson looked up from the TV and locked eyes with Mark. "Well, if you're MI, then you'll find out soon enough."

As Mark walked away, he saw me listening from up on the stairs and mumbled, "Nice guys."

I brushed my teeth in a bathroom that I was pretty sure had never seen the business end of a scrub sponge and slid into bed. I should have enjoyed it more. I was about to get the best night of sleep I would have for six months.

CHAPTER TWO

Our new housemates apparently didn't share my need for a caffeine kick start to each day, a sobering fact I confronted while rooting among the kitchen's empty beer bottles and frozen dinner boxes for some coffee to put in the coffeemaker. But by 0620, Mark and I were in our BDUs (battle dress uniforms, our standard daily camouflage) and had joined a few of the linguists we'd met the night before in a chow hall overlooking the bay for the most respectable pancakes and eggs I'd had in a military facility. The sun was just rising over the water, and despite the previous night's warning signs and the disappointment of not being assigned to the JIG team, I was feeling upbeat about this assignment: six months and out, with valuable experience and contacts gained, and a contribution made.

We met Turk, Ahmad, and several more of our teammates at 19A, where a van would pick us up every morning for the trip to Camp Delta. Turk introduced us to some of the team members who hadn't been at the cookout. It turned out that a linguist I knew from DLI, Dan Eastland, and his wife Vanessa, also DLI, were on the team. They were just twenty-two, married for three years and in the army for four. I hadn't known Dan well, though I'd heard he was a bright and interesting character, and I'd never met Vanessa, but I was glad to see other DLI graduates among us.

Adam Ghazi was a Lebanese American army reservist who'd been living in New York. I would soon find out he was quite a talker, always chatting about his next step in life, either becoming an officer or running his own business. He was obsessed with tae kwon do. Elena Pokrovsky was a quiet MP assigned to the national guard who had been recruited by JDOG when word got out that she was Russian-born and spoke the language fluently. Another surprise—that Russian was needed at the camp. Elena had short, dark hair, dark eyes, and seemed at first a little remote. Mo Bashir, an Egyptian American, was a marine grunt—an infantryman—who'd joined JDOG from Camp Lejeune, North Carolina. Everyone was twentysomething.

Captain Mansur joined us, and I was struck by the fact that Mark and I were the only ones in the group who saluted him, though he clearly didn't mind. This was the loosest command structure I'd ever experienced. The majority of my teammates had no intel training; they were here because they were native speakers. Only Vanessa, Dan, Mark, myself, and two other linguists we hadn't yet met had intelligence training and top secret security clearances. All of the others had been issued hasty temporary clearances, and hadn't gone through the same full-scope security investigation as the DLI people. Mark and I had also taken polygraphs. We were a pretty motley crew of MI-trained Americans who spoke anything other than English imperfectly mixed with foreign-born speakers of Arabic and other languages who had no intel background. Not only that, but as Turk had remarked the night before, the religious makeup of our team was striking: Muslims, Christians of various types, nonbelievers, a Mormon, and an ethnic Jew. It could be a combustible mix, especially for dealing with radical Islamic terrorists.

Mo told Mark and me that the van detailed to our team had been dubbed Rosco for some reason lost among the mysteries of Gitmo well before any of us were on the scene. If Rosco wasn't being used for its principal purpose—getting linguists to and from Camp Delta—we could use it for runs downtown or to the beach. Use of Rosco was a highly prized commodity. The only ones on the team who had a car at the base were Vanessa and Dan, who'd bought a primordial rust bucket with shredded upholstery, a classic of the genre known as Gitmo specials, which were perpetually resold for inflated prices as soldiers came and went.

As I hopped into the backseat, Mo threw me a roll of green duct tape and told Mark and me to use it to cover the names on our uniforms. It hit me that I was about to enter a place where I wouldn't want anyone to know who I was.

"Choose an Arabic name that the detainees can call you for the next six months," Mo said. For simplicity's sake, I went with the name one of my Iraqi instructors had suggested I use at DLI—Basam, which means "one who makes others smile." A little ironic, maybe, given I'd be conversing with men behind bars. But Mark went beyond irony. He wanted to call himself Abu Kafer, or "father of the infidel." The others suggested this was a poor idea.

We turned onto the main road, then into a neighborhood similar to ours but with higher-grade housing, and then up an extremely steep hill, where Vanessa pointed out the old Camp X-ray in the distance to the left. X-ray was where the first detainees had been dumped from January until April of 2002, when Delta opened. It was a jumble of razor wire, with cells open to the elements and buckets in place of toilets. It looked more like an animal shelter in a bad neighborhood than a place to keep people. Images of the detainees huddled there in their orange scrub suits had been seared into the public mind by the early TV footage, and I knew that many people, especially abroad, still thought the detainees were being held at X-ray.

I spotted a huge lizard by the side of the road. Iguanas, it turned out, were a constant danger when driving around Gitmo. Hitting one with a vehicle (not hard to do, given their predilection for broiling themselves on the pavement) could get you a ten-thousand-dollar fine.

Captain Mansur told Mark and me more about the job on the way, explaining that we'd be on twelve-hour shifts, from 0700 to 1900, two days on and then two days off. During the shift, a team of about six of us would sit in a small office near the cellblocks with a few handheld radios. We'd wait for a guard, a psych technician, a medic, or the chaplain to call on the radios and tell us they needed help with a detainee, then we'd go and translate whatever was required. The consolation prize for not being in on interrogations, it appeared, was a much easier schedule than I'd expected. I'd have plenty of time to catch up on reading, hit the pool, work on a tan, and get back in shape at the gym.

Maybe a mile down the road—past other housing clusters, a few low-rise office buildings, and a lot of scrubby open terrain—we came to a set of large cement roadblocks staggered about every fifteen yards on either side of the road so that we had to weave our way through them. The first checkpoint on the approach to Camp Delta was coming up. Two MPs manned the guard shack there in full combat gear: Kevlar flak jacket, belt with two canteens, spare ammunition, and an NBC (nuclear, bio, chemical) mask. They carried loaded M16s.

We all readied our Gitmo-issued IDs, color coded according to clearance level. Mine was orange, for secret. The paperwork for my green top secret badge hadn't yet arrived from Fort Meade. One MP inspected our IDs while the other checked the back of the van. They waved us on and we threaded a few more cement barriers. About fifty yards past the checkpoint to the left, I spotted a barricade of sandbags stacked about eight feet high and thirty feet long—an improvised fighting position. Later I would sometimes see soldiers there with their weapons aimed at the checkpoint, ready to fire on any vehicle that tried to run through.

Finally the barrier around Camp Delta came into view, a twelve-foot high chain-link fence iced with several rows of concertina and barbed wire. The fence was covered with green canvas tarp so you couldn't see in or out. Plywood guard towers jutted up at about thirty-foot intervals, each with an American flag displayed on the side and manned by more soldiers with M16s. A simple, white, wooden sign along the fence read CAMP DELTA: JOINT TASK FORCE GUANTÁNAMO BAY, CUBA. We pulled into the gravel parking lot in front of the camp and started walking toward the gate, our IDs ready.

All the MPs I'd met on base so far, housemates included, seemed pretty unhappy. I couldn't say I blamed them. Many, like the two we were approaching, stood outdoors day after day locking and unlocking gates for entire shifts, and the heat was already overbearing by 0700.

Two thick steel locks, one above the other a few inches apart, secured the gate, which the MP unlocked with two of the gold keys on his softball-sized key ring. He stared blankly at me when I said good morning.

The gate didn't open right into the camp. It led into a square, fenced-in pen with another gate at the far side, about ten yards away. This double-gating system was common throughout the camp. The MP who had just let us in had to lock the first gate before he could walk across to open the second. Meanwhile, another MP checked our bags to make sure no one had a camera or electronic device. I felt as if we were about to face off in one of the WWF's old steel-cage matches.

We went through the second gate and we were in, inside the wire.

The scene in front of me was surreal—again, the Gitmo disconnect. In the distance straight ahead, about half a mile away, stretched the gorgeous vista of the clear blue Caribbean shimmering in the morning sun, the tropical paradise of Guantánamo Bay. But in the near and middle distance lay a Halliburton-built prison camp of drab off-white metal structures resembling double-wide trailers. The ground cover was gravel and dust. A prison camp where a Club Med should have been. The site, though not the structure, had been used to house thousands of Haitian refugees in the early 1990s.

Two long gravel lanes ran toward the water, each about thirty feet wide. Running down the lanes were the slightly elevated trailerlike structures, about half a dozen on each side. Captain Mansur explained to Mark and me that these were the cellblocks holding about six hundred detainees from more than forty nations. They were made from old shipping containers that had been cut in half lengthwise, with the two pieces stuck together end to end. Each cellblock was individually fenced off and had a small fenced asphalt recreation yard, about half the size of a basketball court, and a couple of open-air showers, made of yet more fencing, in the back. On either side of each lane, between it and the cellblocks, ran a narrow fenced-in lane, with gates in front of each block, which was patrolled by MPs.

To get into the whole labyrinth, an MP first had to let you into one of the the wide central lanes through double gates that were smaller versions of the one at Camp Delta's entrance. Then an MP would meet you at the gate in front of the cellblock you were heading for, and let you first into the smaller lane and then into the cellblock area. I could see that the guards must have a great time of it constantly patrolling up and down those lanes, letting people in and out of the blocks. No wonder they were so sullen.

Between the main gate to Camp Delta and the cellblocks was a group of smaller, trailerlike structures and metal huts. Captain Mansur pointed out the medical clinic for the detainees over on our left, and the interrogation and administration buildings in front of us and to our right. Our linguists' office was also to the right. The first cellblock on the left, Captain Mansur told us, was Delta block, where they put the most disturbed detainees because it was closest to the medical clinic. Mark and I glanced at each other, wondering what those guys must be like.

Right away I spotted a detainee being led by a guard to the clinic, wearing the bright orange pants and shirt so familiar from news photos. He was thin and hunched, with long scraggly black hair and a grayish-black beard; his ankles were shackled and his hands cuffed. The MP was holding his arm firmly. I wished I were golfing.

That was the first of a thousand times that I felt as if history was taking a snapshot. I was standing in a place completely unique in the American experience.

Captain Mansur said he wanted Mark and me to give DOCEX—short for document exploitation—a try before we went to work on the cellblocks. DOCEX was where the camp's linguists translated handwritten letters to and from the detainees into English, then passed them to another unit where intelligence analysts would try to determine if the letter writers were attempting to convey coded messages. Doing it well required superior Arabic. I wasn't so sure mine would be up to the job.

Ahmad al Halabi was the mainstay of the DOCEX office. He said he had a backlog so large that a detainee's letter home usually didn't leave the base for months. Mark asked Ahmad if he was the only one working there.

"A couple of the others help sometimes," Ahmad said, "but I'm the only one with a computer, so anyone else has to translate in longhand."

Ahmad explained that he would type the letters into his computer in English as he translated them, which was much faster than writing them out. "Since we're short of computers, the command said I could bring my laptop in, but we haven't been able to get more" he explained. "It tells you how high a priority this is around here."

I had brought my own laptop with me to Gitmo, and I asked if I could bring it in.

"I'm sure they would let you," Ahmad answered. "But make sure you get written permission before you do. I had to sign a bunch of forms and make sure the command was on board before bringing mine in."

Not worth the hassle, I quickly decided. I could just imagine what might happen six months later when I was trying to clear security to leave the island and my computer had been used to translate letters to and from detainees.

Ahmad filled us in on the kinds of letters we'd be reading. Detainees as well as their families often quoted from the Koran, Ahmad said, but usually they also wrote of longing for their loved ones and despaired over their open-ended captivity. I said the job sounded miserably depressing.

"Most of the day," Ahmad responded, "I'm either reading a letter from a ten-year-old boy telling his dad how he'll take care of his mom until they're all together again, or one from a detainee saying how much he misses his family and how badly he is being treated here.

"Sometimes I'll get a letter coming in from a detainee's uncle or cousin encouraging him to 'be strong in his faith.' They remind him 'the greater the suffering, the greater the reward.'"

I could see tension in Ahmad's face. The job was unpleasant enough for anyone, but it had to be much worse for a committed Muslim.

"Why don't you work on the blocks instead?" Mark asked.

"I used to, but that bothered me more, so I thought I'd be better off in here. It was hard to see their suffering. If they are guilty, I certainly don't condone what they've done, but they are still humans."

I suddenly realized I didn't want to be having this conversation, not with someone I'd just met and not before getting my own read on the camp.

"We have old men down there," Ahmad continued. "Men in their fifties and sixties, and we have kids down there. I just wonder if these are really the worst of the worst. So I told Captain Mansur I thought it would be best if I worked somewhere away from the blocks."

I knew Ahmad had arrived four weeks earlier, in mid-November. His air force unit in California had asked him to volunteer, told him his country needed him. They'd promised he'd be gone just ninety days, the normal Gitmo stint for an airman (unlike my six-month assignment). I wondered how much sense it made for Ahmad to be there. He was obviously a true American, having lived in the United States since his teenage years. No doubt he loved his adopted country, but his situation was precarious; he'd been given an interim secret clearance, but no intelligence training, and he seemed unprepared to handle the emotional pressure cooker he'd been sent into. Under normal circumstances, he probably couldn't have obtained a clearance because, as I'd soon find out, he was engaged to a Syrian woman. The intelligence community views close relationships with foreign nationals of countries like Syria as suspect on their face.

Ahmad pointed us to a stack of letters, and Mark and I broke out our dictionaries and went to work. All the letters were handwritten and extremely hard to read, but, fortunately, later in the morning Mark and I escaped when we were called to a briefing for new arrivals by Camp Delta's head psychiatrist.

We listened closely as the psychiatrist explained the need to guard our emotions at the camp, and to be careful that we didn't allow the detainees to manipulate us. He also warned us against developing sympathetic feelings for them. He told us to seek help from a counselor if the stress got to be too much.

That was all the training we would get on the emotional ramifications of working at Gitmo. Forty-five minutes of an army psychiatrist's fancy PowerPoint presentation were supposed to ready us to confront individuals who we'd been told had helped plot the attacks of 9/11 and to deal with the mental states of men undergoing intense interrogation while in captivity on foreign turf. Then again, this was the army way, as I'd experienced it many times before. A specialist would graze a topic, show a few slides, and announce that you had been "trained."

After lunch Captain Mansur asked us what we thought of the psych brief.

"Quite interesting, sir," Mark replied. "I now feel mentally and emotionally prepared to face off with the evildoers."

I was a fairly by-the-book soldier, but I was enjoying Mark's rebellious streak. I wondered if it ever landed him in hot water, but he seemed to have a finely honed sense of how far he could go—either that or the luck of the Irish—because Captain Mansur decided to ignore the sarcasm. He told us we'd be joining the team on the blocks for the afternoon.

Before heading into the linguists' office, I went to grab a soda from the machine outside. While counting out my change, I caught a glimpse of another orange suit shuffling toward an interrogation building. We'd see them coming and going all day long, I realized; I'd better get used to it.

Vanessa was the shift leader on blocks duty. Mo, Turk, and Adam were also on. The linguists' office, one of several rooms in the small structure, was about ten feet by twelve feet and furnished with only a collapsible metal table and a few folding chairs. On one wall hung a whiteboard for keeping track of who was out on which calls, and a small bookcase with a few dictionaries stood in the back. When we walked in, Mo was reading an old issue of *Maxim*.

Mark and I had only been there a few minutes when a call came in. Mo volunteered and told me to come along for the ride. We crunched along the gravel to the gate into one of the two lanes between the blocks. An MP opened the first gate, we went into the enclosure, then he locked up behind us and opened the second one. I said hello, and he looked as though he'd just as soon be poked in the eye with a sharp stick as respond. He kept his head down, his hat low, and mumbled, "Good morning, sergeant."

We walked over to the double gates to cellblock Echo, and another cheery MP let us through. He told us which cell held the detainee who'd called for a translator and told us to "go ahead up."

Showtime.

The metal floor of the cellblock let out a thunderous echo when hit by our highly shined army combat boots. Cells of pale green steel mesh ran the length of the block on either side, with one detainee per cell and a name card affixed to each. The cells were small, six feet eight inches by eight feet, with metal beds fixed to the steel mesh walls, squatting-style flush toilets on the floor, and sinks low to the ground. That, I found out, was to make it easier for the detainees to wash their feet, part of the cleansing ritual before Muslim prayer.

I was about to walk into the midst of nearly fifty men, all bound by an alleged hate for the United States, who I had no doubt would kill me if they had the chance. Some of them may have helped plan the hijacking of those planes, and now I was coming face to face with them.

But first I had to deal with a wicked onslaught of BO. As we walked through the cellblock the stench was unbearable. Most of the detainees didn't even look up, but a few checked me out curiously. I was literally the new kid on the block. I tried to observe them without looking any of them in the eye; I wasn't quite ready. A few of them were studiously reading Korans. Some of the detainees I walked by gazed at me with a weird longing look on their faces, as if I might for some reason be there to help them.

The detainee who had called for us looked like he was in his midthirties. He had a long black beard with spots of gray and a serious case of bed head. He complained that he'd asked more than once to see a doctor but had not been placed on the list. While I listened, testing how much I could understand, another detainee about four cells down started shouting "Mutarjim, mutarjim." Translator, translator.

"Erik, why don't you go see what he wants," Mo said.

"This should be fun," I said, taking a deep breath.

I walked over to the detainee and said, "Ahlan wa sahlan." Hello. Then "Shu inta aayiz?" What do you want?

He was surprised I spoke Arabic. "You are new, where are you from?" he asked. I avoided talking about myself, thinking I should just find out why he'd called and pass the information along.

"Yes, I'm new," I said. "What can I do for you?" I asked, as politely as I thought I should.

"Do you know why I'm here?"

"I can't help you with that; I'm just a translator."

"Where are you from?" he asked.

"What do you want?" I asked back, ignoring his inquiry.

Then he asked, "Is the blonde married?" He was talking about Vanessa, who was popular with the detainees. She was pleasant to them and tried to help resolve their complaints. And frankly, they liked talking to a good-looking American woman—Vanessa was blond, blue-eyed, and extremely busty, a trait that did not go unnoticed among the captives.

I continued to refuse to answer his questions, and when he could tell I was about to walk away, he said, "Ask the librarian to see me."

I didn't know what I'd expected from terrorist captives, but I knew that this wasn't it; this guy clearly just wanted a little diversion. Such exchanges with detainees were typical, Mo told me. They often just wanted to shoot the breeze. If we pressed them about why they'd called, they'd usually say they wanted a new book. Later that morning I went on a call to see a captive named Ziad.

"Assalamu aleilkum," I said as I approached him. Peace upon you.

"Wa aleilkum assalamu," he replied. And upon you, peace.

"What can I do for you?" I asked.

"Do you know why I'm here?"

"I can't help you with that."

"Are you married?"

"No. What do you want?"

"Are you from Texas like George Bush?" he asked.

"No. Look, either you tell me what you want or I'm leaving," I said.

Then, sure enough, "I need a new book. I finished this one."

"I'll tell the librarian," I said as I walked away.

I was surprised by how well my Americanized Arabic had worked so far with the detainees, but I still worried that I'd have difficulty understanding some of the dialects. One question the detainees repeated almost manically that day, and as I'd soon learn, every day, was "Why am I here?"

At 1200 a tape of the noontime call to prayer rang out from loudspeakers, reverberating loudly throughout the camp. It startled me. I was surprised that we'd be making that concession to the religious zealotry of the terrorists. Having had exposure to radical Islam during my time in Cairo, it seemed to me that the camp command was helping to facilitate the terrorists' religious devotion, when I'd expected they'd be cutting these men off from all of that. The lilting wail of the call got under my skin a little, making me edgy.

The practice of Islam permeated the camp. Not only was there the taped call to prayer five times a day, but a stenciled arrow in each detainee's cell pointed toward Mecca, and a prayer mat and a cap and a Koran had been issued to each captive. For anyone who wasn't a practicing Muslim or who'd never been to one of the devout cities of the Middle East, this would be an unnerving atmosphere just on the religious front, let alone the little matter of the detainees' possible links to Al Qaeda.

I remembered Turk's blunt comments the night before about the tensions within our linguists' group, how there was such a mix of religions among us and people getting into theological arguments all the time. I was starting to understand why everyone might be a little tightly wound, and I wondered how the Arab American Muslims on our team must feel, finding themselves among these radicals.

Later that afternoon Vanessa stormed into the room, saying, "These guards are fucking worthless."

"What happened now?" Adam asked.

"One of those assholes crushed a detainee's cookies again before passing him his MRE. All that shit does is make both our jobs harder." Generally the detainees got MREs—meals ready to eat—for their midday chow, like the ones that troops deployed to war zones often lived on, but with the heating devices removed.

I'd picked up on a lot of hostility from the guards, and I asked Vanessa if the MPs typically spent their whole day pissed off. Mo and Vanessa both answered yes at the same time.

"Of course it doesn't help," Vanessa added, "that every day the MP commanders are telling the guards these guys are the very men responsible for 9/11. If I believed that, I would want to crush their cookies too." I wondered how much she knew about the detainees.

At 1900 we got the call saying Rosco had arrived; time for shift change. Vanessa and I were the last ones to climb into the van, sitting in the far back. As the others launched into a heated debate about the coming NFL playoffs, Vanessa asked me what I thought of my first day.

"It's a lot to take in," I said. "I imagine it gets hard hearing them griping every day and constantly asking why they're being held."

"Let me give you some advice, Erik," she said quietly. "You need to guard your emotions here."

She sounded exactly like the PowerPoint psych brief. I asked her what she meant.

"Everyone in this van falls into one of two categories," she said. "Those in one group force themselves to believe that every detainee here was somehow partially responsible for 9/11. That allows them to justify their hatred toward these men and detach themselves emotionally. They're lying to themselves, but it makes their lives easier and their time go by faster."

Vanessa had already been at the camp six months, so I listened closely.

"The other linguists . . . you can see the frustration in their eyes. They become more and more sympathetic every day to the detainees' circumstances. They ponder and argue about whether or not there are innocent men here. They hate the MPs because the MPs hate the detainees. They think the psych techs are idiots. And they believe the doctors don't really care. You'll figure out real quick who's in each group."

One big happy family, I thought to myself.

"My advice, Erik," she concluded, "is to find a happy medium. Don't view each detainee as someone who helped plot 9/11, because it's not true. But at the same time, you can't get emotionally involved when it comes to these men."

I was glad the van was pulling onto our street. Vanessa seemed to be telling me to create an artificial reality in my mind and shut the detainees out. I didn't see how that was going to help in contending with these men. After one day I was already wondering whether my initial impulse to stick only to translating and have as little interaction with them as possible was unwise. Even Vanessa didn't do that. From my perspective, the reason to get to know them a little was simple: Understanding your enemy is essential to defeating him. Terrorism and its motivations were complex, and I didn't think we were going to make much headway if we didn't recognize these guys were multifaceted human beings with views we needed to comprehend so we could combat them effectively.

According to Vanessa and that forty-five-minute psych brief, I was supposed to just shut myself off to the complexities of interacting with the detainees and simply do my job. But even though we unfortunately weren't privy to what the interrogators and linguists on the JIG side were learning, I thought it ought to be possible, and even useful, to gain insight into these guys and their lives without being in the tank for them.

Truth was, the idea of walling myself off from what was happening in front of me took me back to my own emotional badlands. Doing just that had only caused me a lot of painful self-recrimination. It all had to do with my delusions about my marriage. Debbie had not only cheated on me while I was away at basic training, she'd done it even before then. I'd been told about it, but I hadn't wanted to hear the truth. Two days before I left for basic, I'd had a call from one of my closest friends, one of the three Mikes. He said he needed to talk and asked me to come over to his place.

When I got to Mike's, he and another of our group, Timmy, sat me down. They told me that Debbie had slept with two guys we knew and confessed to Mike's girlfriend when she was drunk and feeling guilty.

Mike, Timmy, and I had known each other so long, I knew they had no reason to lie to me. In seventh grade, Tim had been the big man on the basketball team my dad coached; he and I could have produced an instructional video on the model execution of the pick-and-roll. Mike and I had both played in a legendary ninth grade game against Scranton Tech in which he scored 46 points, thus earning the nickname Swelly for what we joked would happen to his head. In the years since, Swell and I had grown extremely close, holding endless two-man symposia at his apartment about the meaning of life. Our talks were facilitated by the trifecta of amenities at his place: keg, pool table, and dartboard. These guys were like family.

Part of me rejected what I'd heard; denial was very appealing when my world was being shattered right before I was shipping out for eight weeks. Debbie and I certainly had our problems, but I had never dreamed that my high school sweetheart, the daughter of a Baptist minister, would sleep around.

Debbie knew I'd gone over to Mike's, and she walked in just after Swell and Tim told me the news. Hell broke loose. She flatly denied all the allegations and said that my friends had never liked her. Deep down I knew she must be lying, but I tried to believe her; maybe my friends had somehow misunderstood things, I told myself.

The next couple of days I acted like everything was fine. When I left for basic, we both acted as if saying good-bye was difficult, and it was—for me. But when I called her from Fort Leonard Wood, she didn't want to have a real conversation and I could hear betrayal in her voice. I learned the extent of her deception when I went home. She had continued cheating with even more guys. I was furious, but I blamed myself as much as I blamed her, for refusing to confront the facts.

I left for DLI just a few days later, and since I'm no good at keeping my emotions to myself, it wasn't long before my close-knit class of ten, and then my instructors, knew everything. When one of my Saudi professors learned of Debbie's infidelities, he was flabbergasted. He called me into his office, then looked me in the eye and said in thickly accented English, "Ya Basam, in my country we would take her to the town square and chop off her head! You should do the same!" He made a chopping gesture with his hand. He wasn't joking.

Beheading not being an option, I filed for divorce, and I promised myself one thing: not to repeat the mistake of trying to make things better by creating some sort of invented world in my head. I had no doubt that doing so would make the complexities of Camp Delta more manageable, but I knew that whatever other options I might choose for coping with the place, tuning out shouldn't be on the list.

Back at home, over a few beers on our cement-slab patio, Mark and I decompressed and compared notes about our first day inside. We passed by our MP roommates on our way out the sliding glass door without ever making eye contact. I was pleased that I'd successfully gone twenty-four hours without speaking to any of them.

Mark twisted the cap off his Miller Lite and said, "Thank God we got out of DOCEX. How about Ahmad?"

"Yeah, he definitely seems stressed."

"No fuckin' shit. And what kind of a strange command is this?"

"Definitely relaxed," I said. "Doesn't seem the best scenario given that most of us aren't even trained to be here."

"That's a fucking understatement!" Mark took a long slug

of beer, put his bottle down on the cement, and looked me square in the eye.

"I've already decided this place is a fucking nuthouse!" An awkward moment of silence followed.

"I need another beer," he said.

I stared out at the shadows of the falling night. I was worried about the loose command structure and the lesser accountability I knew went along with being on an ad hoc team versus a regular army unit. Young and vulnerable IAs—individual augmentees, or soldiers who were sent on assignment away from their home unit—in an environment as highly stressed as Gitmo's, with all their support structure stripped away, could feel very alone. Alone was the last thing you wanted to be at Gitmo, I'd already realized.

The night darkened as we sprawled on our rickety lawn chairs, drank our beers, and shot the shit. We didn't have much of a view—beyond our little yard was a wide expanse of fenced-in field where it was rumored nuclear missiles used to be buried. I had no idea if that was true; probably not. But Gitmo's history, its present—hell, the very existence of the place—made the unlikely seem possible.

CHAPTER THREE

"M utarjim, mutarjim!" Even if we were walking among terrorists, it did something for the ego to be so sought after. As I made my way down Charlie block one morning I was barraged as usual by calls for my services.

"Jundi!" Soldier.

"Mutarjim!" Translator.

I headed straight for cell 36, whose occupant had called for assistance.

I'd been sitting in the office with Adam and Mo, who was bitching as usual about the shortage of attractive single women at Gitmo. He often did that when Vanessa wasn't around, and she was at the clinic that morning translating for one of the base doctors. When the first call came in, I grabbed my sunglasses and offered to take it. I was happy for a diversion from being reminded that I was without Darcie for six months.

As I got to cell 36, I checked the card out front and saw that the detainee's name was Habib. He had shorter hair than most, though dark as usual, and dark brown eyes, and he was sitting Indian style on the floor.

"Assalamu aleilkum," I said to him.

"Wa aleilkum assalamu," he replied.

This was a good sign, an indication that he might not be combative.

I asked him what he needed. The night before, he told me, his interrogator had promised that he would be allowed to move to a different cell. But when the morning guard shift arrived, they didn't move him, and he wanted to know why.

I told him to wait (as if he was going anywhere—I'd have to stop saying that) while I asked the guards about it. The NCOIC (noncommissioned officer in charge) said there was nothing in his notes for the day about moving Habib.

Maybe Habib was lying—always a possibility with these guys—or the interrogator may have made the promise but forgot to tell the guards, or possibly the night guards forgot to tell the day shift. "Either way," said the MP, "he isn't getting moved unless I hear it from his interrogator or my superiors."

I headed back to 36. "I wish I could help you, Habib," I said. "But today's not your lucky day. The guards say they don't know anything about moving you. You'll have to talk to your interrogator."

"But I won't see that bitch until next week," he shouted. "She knows that I am innocent. I'm telling her everything I know. I should get my reward. I'm stuck here with all these idiot Afghanis!"

Either by accident or by the interrogators' design, Habib, an Arabic-speaking Yemeni, was surrounded by non-Arab Pashtuns and Dari-speaking Afghan detainees. Arabs consider themselves higher up the food chain than Afghanis. Their cultures, if not their religions, are very different.

The closest Arab was six cells down and Habib said of him, "He is Al Qaeda and I don't want to talk to him and make anyone think I'm one of them." I had no idea if he was telling the truth, but I repeated that I couldn't help him.

"You don't understand," he yelled. "I can't stay in this cell. I'm going crazy. These fools around me are driving me insane! You have to help me!"

"Habib, even if I wanted to help you, I couldn't." I was getting annoyed. What if the interrogator really had meant for him to be moved? But then, as had been made abundantly clear to me, that wasn't my business and there was nothing I could do other than pass on his complaint to the MP, which I'd already done.

The first day's briefing had warned us to watch what we promised the detainees. I started to walk away.

"Hamar!" Habib shouted.

He had just called me an ass. I wheeled around. "What did you say?"

"The blond girl would have helped me."

"Listen to me carefully," I snapped at him. "You need to wake up fast. Fair or unfair, you are *not* in a hotel. You are being held in an American jail."

Whoa. I was spouting the company line. The guards loved the you're-not-in-a-hotel message.

I had been nonchalant when Dar told me she worried that this assignment would change me. "I'm not going off to war in Iraq; I'm just going to Cuba to translate," I had said. She wasn't buying it. "Either you think I'm dumb or you're naive," she'd shot back. "Do you really think you're going to spend six months seeing people in chains and talking to terrorists face to face without feeling an impact?" "Dar," I'd assured her, "I'm trained for this." Right. I'd expected that each day into the new job would be easier. Instead, each day became more complicated than the day before.

"Send the blond girl!" Habib shouted as I walked away, ignoring the clamor of calls for "Mutarjim!" and "Jundi!" from the other Arab detainees on the cellblock. I made sure the guard understood Habib's problem, and he thanked me for coming down and said he'd put it in his notebook.

This was one in the playbook of common detainee encounters. They would want something—library books, a cell change, different food, to know when they would ever meet with a lawyer—and they would string the conversation out, or turn hostile when we said we couldn't help them.

Life for detainees inside the wire was mundane at best, except of course when they were in interrogation. Though at times they became animated—sometimes much too animated, as I was soon to experience—for the most part they simply sat cross-legged on their beds or the floor and read, or stared blankly with an empty look on their faces. The highlights of their day were two hot halal, or religiously correct, meals and the MRE—probably better than they'd get at home, but not much to look forward to. They had several recreation and shower periods per week; the number and length depended on what category their interrogators decided to put them in—one, two, or three.

Level three was for detainees who had just arrived or weren't cooperating with their interrogators. They were given only the basics: a blanket, a prayer mat and cap, a Koran, a toothbrush. Level two was for moderately cooperative detainees and generally included perks like a drinking cup and perhaps greater access to library books. Level one was for the best Gitmo citizens. They were afforded everything the others got plus extra rec yard and shower time, magazines, even games like checkers, which they could play with adjacent captives who could look through the mesh and tell them where to move their pieces. Even those small items made a world of difference to them.

Detainees were allowed to kick soccer balls around their cellblock rec yards, but only one detainee was allowed in the yard at a time, so there was nobody to kick it back. Besides, there weren't enough balls for every rec yard, which became a bone of contention. In the blazing Cuban sun, the blocks, which didn't have any air-conditioning, could be brutally hot. There was a ventilation system on each cellblock that was supposed to be turned on if the temperature rose to 85 or higher, but that often didn't happen.

After a few days, I could tell when detainees had just returned from a tough interrogation. They often had a defeated look: head held low and eyes lifeless. Sometimes it was more obvious; they'd sit huddled in a fetal position in the corner of their cells, staring off into space or even quietly crying.

Occasionally they'd come back and start boasting loudly about how they had said nothing to their interrogators and how they had duped them. Many of the linguists suspected the boasts were overcompensation and that those guys were spilling. Clearly, some of the detainees were under a good deal of psychological stress.

One quiet morning, shortly after I'd gulped down some runny army scrambled eggs, a female air force officer with green eyes and short brown hair walked into our office and said, "Who is my victim today?"

Since I was the newest member of the team, and Mo was engrossed in the latest issue of *FHM* magazine, he said, "Erik, why don't you go be the detainees' shrink today?"

I was puzzled. "What kind of trouble are you guys sending me into?" I asked. Turned out that Jessica was one of the psych techs in the camp.

"She has the noble role of trying to ensure as few of the detainees as possible attempt to off themselves on any given day," Vanessa threw in. I'd already heard that there were lots of suicide attempts among the detainees, maybe as many as one a week, and a linguist was usually called to the scene. Fortunately, I hadn't been on one of those calls yet. I grabbed my hat and sunglasses and followed Jessica out the door.

The first detainee we talked to was Said. When we approached his cell, he was sitting cross-legged in the front corner, looking around a little strangely, observing everything around him. He almost appeared to be in a trance. Jessica said, "Good morning, Said" and I dutifully translated.

"How are you sleeping?" she asked.

"Fine," he said, without even looking our way.

"How are you eating?"

"Fine."

"Are you having any nightmares?"

"No."

"Do you feel hopeless?"

"No."

"Are you thinking about hurting yourself or others?"

"No."

With that, we were done with Said. On to the next detainee. This same routine was repeated over and over again as I followed Jessica around through the cellblocks. She'd write observations about each detainee in her little green notebook. As we approached one man, he began reciting, without ever looking up from his Koran, "I'm sleeping well, I'm eating well, I don't have nightmares, and I don't want to hurt anyone, including myself. This place is paradise." He had the rituals of paradise down.

Seemed to me that asking these men if they were feeling hopeless was a little absurd, given their situation. That's exactly what the interrogators wanted them to feel. It was a little ridiculous that the psych team was trying to conduct damage control for everything the interrogators were trying to do, and I found that, in fact, there were certain detainees the psych techs didn't see because the interrogators wanted those guys depressed and dejected.

Jessica told me that some detainees claimed they were seeing evil spirits, which they called djinns, and had been put on meds. The detainees spoke to the djinns, who taunted them, but they wouldn't open up about them with the psych techs. They wanted to talk only with the chaplain, Captain James Yee, a Muslim who advised the camp's leadership about religious issues regarding the detainees. To them the spirits were religious visitations, and very real. Most of the detainees believed in them.

Three things helped the detainees get through the tedium of the blocks and the stress of endless hours of interrogation: their faith, their brothers—though not all of them got along, not by a long shot—and whatever conversation, chaos, and altercations with their captors they could create, watch, or participate in. Islam was their primary source of strength, and I had to admit that in these circumstances, their devotion was impressive. The extreme nature of their beliefs, however, and the notion that we might actually be hardening those beliefs, was troubling. Mo had told me that many of the library's religious books—by far the most popular volumes—were quite fundamentalist in perspective. If the detainees weren't radicals when they got there, there was a good chance they would be when they left—*if* they left.

Most of them wanted to be martyrs for Allah. Nearly all of them prayed five times daily; fasted at least during the designated periods of the Islamic calendar, if not more often; and had memorized portions of the Koran—a few could recite the entire book.

Within each cellblock certain detainees would take on special roles. Usually there were a couple of men most of the others looked up to, often because they were charismatic religious teachers. These teachers took on the part of detainee leaders on the block, a role I would come to understand better as the days wore on. One high-priority detainee was reputedly an Al Qaeda facilitator. These operatives helped with logistical planning, transferred money around, and arranged for safe houses, among a whole range of activities. His specialty was said to be below-the-radar Internet communication. He was young, but had the entire Koran memorized and was a mesmerizing teacher. The detainees were being moved from cellblock to cellblock all the time, shuffled around, but no matter where this individual was transferred, he gained instant respect. Within days he'd be giving afternoon Koranic lectures to the entire block, and while he taught, you could hear a pin drop.

Other detainees would play the role of encouragers, counselors of a sort. If an encourager knew someone was undergoing intense interrogations, he would urge him to resist temptation and fight the Kafer—the infidel. I'd hear a detainee in this role calling out, "You must stay strong, brother. Your reward is yet to come," and quoting verses from the Koran. Still other detainees would take on the role of liaison with the MPs, an unenviable job given the general pleasure with which the MPs listened to detainee complaints. These detainees did the leaders' bidding.

The detainees' reliance on each other clearly proved an effective obstacle for the interrogators. When I was on the blocks, I would often hear detainees proudly referring to their interrogators as stupid, or proclaiming that "I just talk to them so I don't have to be in here with you idiots," jokingly referring to their fellow captives. But the relationship between the detainees and interrogators was obviously a good deal more complicated than that. Within my first few days I heard a detainee say he was falling in love with his interrogator, and he sounded so sincere that it was impossible to tell whether he was being sarcastic. I also overheard a detainee complain about how his interrogator was trying to "spiritually manipulate him." At the time, I didn't really understand what that meant.

Whatever controversy the detainees managed to create, they united behind it, and they loved to stir things up. On one of my first days, a detainee leader argued with an MP—through the services of one of my fellow linguists—about when lunch was going to be served. When the MP walked away, the detainee shouted "Allah al-Akbar"—God is great—until he had the entire cellblock chanting with him. It went on for fifteen minutes.

Few issues were as weighty or generated as much agitation within the cellblocks and among camp personnel as the handling of the Koran. Every detainee got a copy if he wanted it, and practically all of them treated it with reverence. Studying their Korans, which were covered in white cloth, occupied most of their day. Any mishandling of the sacred books was not only a personal insult but an insult to Islam itself.

The problem was that the detainees fervently objected to non-Muslims handling their Korans. This presented a huge quandary, since the guards needed to inspect the cells regularly for security reasons, and almost every cell had one. Captain Yee had persuaded the leadership to appease the captives on this point. Whenever an MP needed to inspect a Koran, a Muslim soldier had to be called to do it, which usually meant a linguist. When the MPs radioed us requesting a Muslim interpreter, we knew what the deal was.

But because the policy never made it into writing, it was vague and much debated among intelligence personnel and the MPs, who felt it undermined their authority. So sometimes an MP inspected a Koran himself, which would stir the detainees into a near riot, complete with spitting at the guard and loud choruses of "Allah al-Akbar." These disturbances were a way for them to fight their oppressors—and sometimes a pure source of entertainment. Their capacity to create tension in the camp was great, and they knew it.

The intense hatred for Americans that was festering in the cellblocks was another bond for the captives. Not all of them harbored it, but we were always on guard. Though the detainees sometimes lashed out at the linguists, they saved most of their tauntings for the MPs, who walked up and down the cellblocks, supposedly laying eyes on each detainee every thirty seconds. They were spit at; doused with water, urine, or feces; and called *ibn sharmoota*, "son of a whore." Most of the MPs were army reservists, and I wondered how prepared they were for an assignment like this.

Meanwhile, the only punishment the guards were supposed to impose was removing some comfort item—an extra blanket or prayer oil, maybe—or placing the offending detainee in solitary, which was a dubious disciplinary option at best. The solitary cells had solid metal walls, so the detainee couldn't see out, but they were air-conditioned, and some of the detainees thought of going to solitary as quiet time to read the Koran and reflect. "Maybe I'll throw something at the guard today,"

I'd once heard a captive say, "so I can spend some time in the other cells."

The MPs clearly resented that they had so little control over detainee treatment. That was in the hands of the interrogators, though over time the MPs found their own ways to assert power. If an interrogator didn't want a detainee punished, it couldn't happen—end of story. The intelligence side viewed the detainees as potential information assets, from whom even one little revelation might help piece together a puzzle. The MPs just thought the detainees were treated too well; they were terrorists, responsible for 9/11, and their lives should be miserable. When I reported to a guard one day in my first couple of weeks that a detainee claimed his interrogator had promised him an additional blanket, the MP spit back at me, "I don't give a shit what some interrogator says. They're the ones screwing up this mission."

The guards did have one weapon in their small arsenal. If a detainee was adamantly resisting a command, they could go to their nuclear option and summon a squad of five MPs—called an IRF team, for Initial Reaction Force—which would subdue the captive with brute strength. Though I hadn't seen one in action, I'd heard they were highly effective and quite something to witness.

The MPs were on their best behavior when the International Committee of the Red Cross was paying one of its periodic visits. They, as well as the linguists, weren't supposed to talk to the Red Cross representatives unless absolutely necessary. The leadership was very wary of them, telling us to watch what we said when we went by the organization's trailer, which was parked just outside the perimeter of the camp. When a Red Cross staffer was meeting with a detainee on a cellblock, he or she would usually leave when we strode into view; they considered their conversations with the captives absolutely confidential. In return for access to the camp, the group wasn't supposed to speak publicly about what it saw. If it had any complaints about conditions or treatment of the detainees, they were conveyed directly to the government. That was their general arrangement worldwide.

If the MPs had to behave around the Red Cross, they certainly never felt as if they had to do so around us. As fraught with tensions as the relationship between the guards and the interrogators was, the guards reserved a special loathing for linguists. They didn't trust us because only we could understand what the detainees were saying, and they tended to think of us as sympathizers, a term at Gitmo that included anyone who betrayed any signs of compassion or empathy for the captives, or talked to them a little too long. Once you were labeled a sympathizer by one of the guards, you had at most a few days before all of them were scrutinizing you when you went on calls. Some guards believed that they needed to keep an eye on us in case we tried to pass anything to, or take anything from, the detainees. They thought we should just get in and out of their cellblocks quickly, with as little said as possible. An MP who saw me laughing at a detainee's joke once glared at me and said, "What the fuck is wrong with you; are you one of them detainee lovers?"

Vanessa said she'd sometimes complained to an NCOIC, the enlisted officer who took care of the day-to-day, on-the-ground business for each MP unit's commander, about the guards' lack of attention to the detainees' medical problems. He didn't want to hear it. She cited the case of a captive on Sierra block who had complained of back pain each time she saw him and asked to see a doctor. Each time, she'd told the MPs responsible for the block. They were supposed to put the request for a doctor in their daily log.

After three weeks of this, she finally asked the NCOIC why the detainee hadn't seen a doctor yet. He told her the detainee's welfare was none of her concern. She responded that it might be of more concern to some of his superiors and said further, "I want to know if these complaints have ever been logged."

"Listen, bitch," he responded, "I run this cellblock the way I see fit. If I think a detainee is complaining about back pain just to get to walk across the camp to the medical clinic one sunny afternoon, then I'm not going to put it in my log. Now leave my block and next time, stay in your lane."

"Stay in your lane" is common military parlance for "butt out." In combat, it means to maintain your own lane of fire.

Of course, as Vanessa had said, the guards' leadership constantly reminded them to view the detainees with total contempt. I would sometimes hear their briefings as I returned to the camp from lunch and passed the 1400 shift getting ready to go on duty. Their commander was an all-business, tough-as-nails lieutenant colonel. "Always remember," he would say, "you guys should feel privileged to be here guarding this scum. These men are the worst of the worst. This place is reserved for those terrorists who either helped plan 9/11 or were planning future attacks against us when they were apprehended."

When I arrived at Gitmo, the MP unit guarding the detainees had recently rotated. The new unit was the 902nd MP detachment from the Connecticut National Guard. One staff sergeant in particular, Ed Pagnotti, seemed to have inordinate influence over the behavior of his fellow guards. Pagnotti was an army reservist and police officer in New York City. He no doubt felt a special contempt for the detainees for that reason. I'm sure he felt a strong bond with the officers and firefighters who lost their lives in the attacks. He used to stop by the linguists' office just to say hi every few days, but I soon learned that getting Pagnotti in any conversation pertaining to the camp was a mistake. Though he was genuinely friendly with the linguist team, he said straight out that he thought we were all sympathizers. He'd often comment about how well we treated the detainees and, as he put it one afternoon, how he couldn't believe "we can't beat the fuck out of these terrorist shitbags."

Although most of the MPs thought we were way too indulgent with the detainees, our relationship with them was much more tangled. The detainees thought of the linguists as their primary source of hope. We were their link to the outside world, their decoder rings for understanding what was going on—as if we understood it—and their way to make themselves heard. It was a unique connection, one the guards and interrogators didn't really fathom. And the detainees did everything in their power to lean on, soften, or connect with us. We had to be wary, and they could say some crazy things to us.

Sometimes they seemed to be trying to suck up to me; sometimes they just made me laugh. One afternoon a detainee said, "Hey, soldier, you seem like you must know a lot. When are we getting out of this place?" Then there was the guy who said, "The blond girl likes me; we talk all the time. If I can get her to sleep with you, can you get me a lawyer?"

Mustapha, a Syrian who claimed to have been in Afghanistan working as a missionary, was an unwavering Islamist but was intensely curious about Christianity. Whenever I saw him on Echo block, he'd ask me questions about my religion.

"Do you really believe Jesus Christ was God?"

"Yes."

"But I thought Jesus was the son of God."

"In Christianity he's both."

"That doesn't make sense."

"It's one of those matters of faith, Mustapha."

We always spoke in hushed tones because he didn't want his compadres to hear him asking religious questions of an infidel. He was astonished to meet an American with any religious beliefs at all because he viewed the United States as a pagan country where men cared only about alcohol, money, and chasing women.

Mustapha was confounded when I explained to him that Christians' motivation to do right comes from their gratitude for God's love and forgiveness, rather than fear of judgment alone. This was incomprehensible to him. He didn't believe in a loving God, nor did he know if he was assured paradise. He genuinely hoped the Americans would kill him so he could be certain of becoming a true martyr.

Often the detainees' efforts to connect were completely innocent—they *liked* to converse with American soldiers. But in other instances they were playing at pure manipulation.

They wanted the linguists to be sympathetic, to know their family situation, to believe that they actually loved the United States. They were hoping for an ally on the inside. If we occasionally didn't know the difference, they rarely realized how powerless we were. We could sometimes iron out misunderstandings or help in some other small way, but to adopt the role of problem solver or counselor was to tread on quicksand, and usually to sink. The camp watchwords were: "Get them to tell all to their interrogators, that's where all their hope should be placed. Don't act as though anyone else can help them."

The linguist team members tended to deal with the strain of all of this in different ways. Some just kept quiet, barely talked about the camp, and always changed the subject when controversy arose. Others, like Mark and Vanessa, talked about it constantly. Some seemed to love to disagree with one another about the place, almost relishing arguments. And there were a few who were extremely irritated by the detainees' very existence and would lash out at them.

Mark, who almost immediately had become a close confidant, was mostly just curious about the whole system. He tried to appease the MPs as much as possible, but he also talked to the detainees more than the rest of us, debating with them over religious issues and challenging them on their views. "I'm trying to be nice to these MPs," he said to me one night over beers, "but I think they can tell I find the detainees interesting, and that bugs 'em."

I tried to avoid talking too much about what I thought yet. The shift schedule made the job tolerable, those two days on, two days off, and I started going to the pool, about a mile's walk from my house, as well as the gym. But even so, after just a couple of weeks I could feel the emotional toll the place was taking.

The day before Christmas Eve, at 0930, I found myself on the other side of a cell door from a Saudi sitting at the edge of his steel bed in Sierra block. I peered at him through my Oakleys—technically verboten for on-duty soldiers because of the oval brand symbol on them—and noted that he had that blank look I'd seen often on detainees, the one that gave the impression they were becoming numbed out. Once he started speaking, though, his expression changed and I knew that he wasn't numb, he was emotionally distraught.

"I just wanted someone to talk to," Wael said. "I need your help." He spoke pleadingly.

"I'm not sure if I can help you, but I'll listen. What's up?"

"I don't belong here. I—"

Immediately I cut him off. "Listen, there's nothing I can do about that. Whatever information you have regarding what happened to you before you came here you must discuss with your interrogator." That was the by-the-book response I used with any detainee who acted as though I could do more than help him get some ibuprofen.

The corners of Wael's eyes were moist, and I didn't know whether to be angry or to pity him. It was already hotter than hell, I was stationed in this stressed-out funhouse next to an ocean I couldn't enjoy, my family and friends were doing last-minute Christmas shopping, and some fucking terrorist was crying and asking me to help him. How the hell did I get into this?

But there was something about this guy that kept me from walking away. Was I letting my guard down? Was it the effect of the holidays? I was certainly curious about some of these characters.

Wael was staring at me. I knew I should head back to the office, but I stood and looked this man squarely in the eye for what seemed like endless awkward seconds. Finally, he said, "If I accept that you are unable to help me, will you stay and listen to my story?" After no small internal debate, I took off my sunglasses, looked at Wael, and said, "I'll listen if you fully understand that I am helpless."

"I understand," Wael said. "Alf shukr." A thousand thank-yous.

"Afwan," I said. You're welcome. "I'm listening."

"I just want someone to understand," he said softly but urgently. "I've been here a year, my interrogator knows my story, and he hasn't spoken to me in four months. As a matter of fact, I have probably only spoken with him five times. I was turned over to the Americans in Afghanistan, but I am a Saudi," he said.

"What were you doing in Afghanistan, Wael?" I asked.

"Good question, Basam. I know the American authorities think that every Arab in Afghanistan was training to be a terrorist, but this is not true. There were many Arabs there who had nothing to do with terrorism. And do you know how they ended up here?"

"No, I don't, Wael. I assume you were either picked up on the battlefield or you were affiliated with an Al Qaeda training facility."

"No no no, this is not true, Basam. If they are telling you this, it is a lie. Do all the soldiers here believe this?"

"Why don't you just tell me how you got here, Wael. Why did you leave Saudi Arabia?"

Wael began his story. His father, he said, was a university professor in Riyadh. He, too, had a university degree, but he couldn't get a job when he graduated. In the late nineties he went to Afghanistan to work in an orphanage. He met a woman, married her, and had three children—two boys and a girl. Then he left the orphanage and worked for a farmer. "I had a good life, Basam. I had a good life. I didn't like the Taliban, but they didn't bother me. And I didn't bother anyone. I had never heard of Al Qaeda before I got to this place."

I was suspicious, but asked him to explain how he'd gotten to Guantánamo.

"I was living in a village outside Kandahar when we saw the large American planes flying in the area. We had no idea what was going on, no idea why the Americans were coming to take over. Days later the Northern Alliance moved in and took away every Arab man in the area in addition to some Afghanis of fighting age. They took us to their own prison for a few days, which made this place look like a palace.

"For three days they tortured us," Wael continued. "I watched one man get sodomized. Another man got a beating that nearly killed him. They gave us very little water and very little food."

His voice grew even softer.

"Finally, we were turned over to the Americans and sent to Bagram," he continued. "I was questioned by American interrogators who barely spoke Arabic. I told all of them that I was not a terrorist, but they kept asking me things like, Where are the safe houses? Now I'm hearing rumors that the American authorities were paying the Northern Alliance for each Arab they turned over. Is that true?"

As I listened to Wael, I found I couldn't help but allow myself to wonder. I sometimes wish I hadn't. I would have slept much easier if I had stayed in a personal cocoon. Vanessa had been right about that, at any rate. One side of me was saying this guy was full of shit; the other was saying, what if?

"Wael," I said, "I know you wanted to tell me your story, but there is really nothing I can do."

"Basam, I miss my children. They have no idea why their father is gone. How do I explain this to them?"

"What do you want me to say, Wael?"

"I just wanted you to know; I want anyone who will listen to know. I believe that you cannot help me. I just want you to know. Don't believe all the lies they are feeding you, Basam. Not every detainee here is a terrorist. Just ask some of the men who haven't seen their interrogators in months."

I had noticed that many of the detainees never seemed to go to interrogations, and I wondered why this was the case. We linguists had heard many similar stories of detainees' being seized by the Northern Alliance, an ad hoc confederation of anti-Taliban militia and warlords with whom the United States had formed a loose and strictly expedient partnership in the war in Afghanistan. Recent press reports had indicated that the United States was paying bounties for terror suspects, and American officials had made reference to this happening as well. It was a troubling piece of information. We all knew people who would turn in their own grandmother for the right sum, and five thousand dollars went a long way in a place like Afghanistan.

It was definitely time to cut this off. "Wael, I have to get going," I said. "You take care of yourself." I put my sunglasses back on and stepped away from the cell. As I turned to head down the corridor, he said, "Ya Basam."

I looked back to see Wael's eyes again filling with tears.

"Yarhamuka Allah." God bless you.

"Wa yarhamuka Allah, Wael," I said. And you also, Wael.

Later that night, after some dinner in front of the TV, Wael's story nagged at me. I wasn't necessarily convinced it was true, although he sounded believable. But the very possibility that he could be right, the notion that I could be contributing to this man's wrongful detention, bugged me.

Ahmad had mentioned his doubt that all the detainees at the camp were really terrorists on my very first day inside, but until that conversation with Wael, I'd been able to put the issue pretty effectively out of my head.

I had tried not to think about the holidays. I'd only been away a couple of weeks, after all, and I knew I was lucky to have managed to reach the age of twenty-seven, with several of those years in the army, without spending a single Christmas away from my family. There were thirty or so of my relatives all within about ten minutes of one another in our part of northeastern Pennsylvania, and normally on Christmas Eve we'd all gather at my aunt's house, exchange gifts, and go to the eleven o'clock candlelight service at our church.

When I woke up on Christmas Eve, I couldn't get that conversation with Wael out of my mind, or the fact that I wished like hell I was with my family in Clarks Summit. I got up, took a run, and headed to the gym, pressing the pounds with Rage Against the Machine, Limp Bizkit, Godsmack plugged into my ears. After lunch I finished *Tuesdays with Morrie* sitting by the pool (a mistake; made me think too much about home). Mark got home around 1915, and we shared a few beers and a frozen pizza on the back patio, talking about what we'd be doing if we were in the States. Mark said he'd probably be in Boston visiting his mom.

He was much more of a loner than I was. He'd grown up with a mother on welfare and no stable father figure. When he was sixteen, he'd beaten the crap out of his mother's boyfriend, who had gotten soused and thrown his mom around the house once too often, Mark said. His mother sided with the boyfriend, though, and helped the authorities prosecute Mark. A judge told him to choose the army or prison.

Mark was really bright, and he had been accepted at MIT by the time the judge ruled. But the tough delinquent from South Boston took the army's test to see if he qualified to become a linguist. He aced it, and later got outstanding scores in Arabic.

This all helped explain Mark's antiauthority streak. He

didn't mind pissing off his supervisors, but he knew when to stop. Yet with most people Mark was a hell of a nice guy. If you were tempted to feel sorry for him, he wouldn't let you. He was much too positive. He'd pulled his life together and he felt great that he'd done so. Along the way he'd been born again, which probably accounts for why he liked to discuss religious issues with the detainees. His interest in them didn't give him any special qualms about their fate, though.

Out on the patio Mark sensed my homesickness, saying, "Sure it's Christmas Eve, but we could be plenty worse places than this, Saar. Look at the situation those six hundred schleps find themselves in tonight. Now that would suck."

"What do you think about all this, Mark?" I asked him. "I mean, you talk with those guys more than anyone; how do you feel?"

"What do you mean; are you talking about the whole legal thing, or how some guys were picked up by the Northern Alliance, or what?"

"The whole thing. The camp, how the guys got here, how they're treated. I want your take on the two weeks," I said.

"Listen to me, Erik," he said, "the difference between you and me is this: you're an idealist, and I'm a realist. I can tell that there's this side of you that believes the United States always must do the 'right' thing; I'll bet you are also the kind of guy who always wants to see the underdog win. You probably cheer for the underdog in every fucking game you watch. Look, bro', if some shit happens here and some of these guys get stuck here for a while, so be it. That stuff is for the bigwigs in Washington to decide."

Christmas Day, Mark and I both worked the usual twelve-hour shift. A few detainees actually wished me a merry Christmas. Lunch at the chow hall was turkey, mashed potatoes, yams, cranberry sauce—the works. Back at the housing unit, I opened my gifts from Darcie: a shirt, a huge package of homemade cookies, a diving watch for the underwater exploring I hoped to do.

I was thinking about home again. Every year that I could remember, our candlelight service had concluded at midnight with my dad singing "O Holy Night." Now, on that holiday night in a tropical detention camp, I couldn't get the second verse out of my head:

Truly he taught us to love one another
His law is love and his gospel is peace
Chains shall he break, for the slave is our brother
And in his name, all oppression shall cease.

I was frustrated that Islamic radicals, in the name of faith, had forced us into this war on terror, which also was becoming a war of religion, and one in which there might be all too many innocent victims.

I'd drawn a great deal of strength in my life from my upbringing in the Christian faith. Churchgoing was an all-day event on Sunday for my family, with Bible study and youth group. Every Wednesday night my parents had choir practice. At some point in my adolescence, my family's faith had become my own. I had even considered going into the ministry, and during my first two years of college I'd studied theology in preparation. Although I ultimately chose a different route, I kept my faith close to heart.

Now I was celebrating Christmas among accused terrorists, reflecting on my beliefs. When I'd first arrived, I'd been taken aback by our playing the call to prayer for the detainees five times a day; that night I could have used a call to prayer of my own. It took only two weeks of immersion in the camp to understand how important it was for the detainees to keep up their religious practice; we owed them that right. Religious liberty was one of our founding principles. What kind of Americans would we be if we denied them that? I knew that if I were locked in that camp, I'd be praying to God day and night, going deep inside my faith to stay strong. I thought that night about how much I wished I was taking part in a service, and how every day, five times a day, the detainees were. We would never prevail in the war on terror by fighting it as a holy war, that was for sure. I'd seen how tenaciously the detainees rallied around Islam.

And what about the Muslim linguists? What must it be like for them to find themselves imported to this devout Islamic environment, I wondered? What kind of strange journey of faith must those guys be having, men like Chaplain Yee, Captain Mansur, and Ahmad al Halabi? I'd heard they were beginning to hold regular services together, along with some of the devout Muslims on the JIG team, and I realized this might have been the first time in their military lives they'd engaged in anything like that kind of group practice of their religion on base. How incongruous. They'd been hastily plucked from bases all over the country simply because they were native Arabic speakers, and here they were facing Muslim detainees whose practice of their religion permeated the camp, steeping these linguists, as they'd probably never been before, in the rituals of their faith. I'd noticed the MPs were especially hostile to the Muslim linguists, and the detainees mostly showed them contempt as well, calling them traitors.

Darcie had warned me that I wouldn't leave this place as the same person, and I was starting to realize how right she'd been.

CHAPTER FOUR

No one on base was in an especially good mood between Christmas and New Year's. There were daily reminders of the holiday season and our friends and families back home. The 90-degree-plus heat didn't do much for holiday spirit. It was worse for the guards and psych techs who had to deal with the detainees' complaints and antics. The captives were pushing Pagnotti's MP unit to see what they could get away with. Maybe they were just trying to make our holiday as miserable as possible, but it seemed to me that some of them had really reached the end of the rope.

Many would soon be marking the one-year anniversary of their captivity at Guantánamo, and there was no light at the end of that tunnel. In November 2001, President Bush had signed a controversial order establishing a whole new system of justice for charging, prosecuting, and punishing non-U.S. citizens he was calling enemy combatants. Yet none of the detainees had yet been charged or allowed to see a lawyer, and the open-endedness of their detention was without question the hardest thing for them to take.

We clearly had some bad actors in the camp; I'd found that out soon enough, although we in JDOG didn't have much information about who they were. But I had to wonder about not charging them formally. Others seemed to have more dubious terrorist credentials. One detainee had told me, "Yes, I was a conscript for the Taliban; I had to fight when they came and told me the Americans were coming. They would have killed me otherwise. But now, I just want to know what my sentence is—five years? Ten years? Will I die here? I just want someone to tell me how long. Your country is supposed to stand for freedom and justice, but we are getting nothing." The detainee population numbered more than six hundred.

Of course, this sense of hopelessness was created by design. The captives were supposed to believe that the only way to end their internment was through complete cooperation with their interrogators, the only catch being that some of those who seemed most tormented by their indefinite stay were those who weren't being interrogated.

On one of those maddening end-of-the-year mornings, Mo asked Mark and me to head over to Foxtrot block. He wouldn't tell us what was going on. We found medics and members of the mental health team waiting for us by the metal stairs leading to the cellblock. The NCOIC gathered us together and told us that the detainees of Foxtrot were about to get their flu shots. This was a public health issue, he said, and every detainee in the camp would get a shot, willingly or not.

I sensed trouble. The reaction of the camp population to the prospect of getting shots wasn't likely to be positive. The captives thrived on conspiracy theories. We had one detainee who didn't even trust us enough to believe the arrow in his cell was pointed toward Mecca. He used to face the opposite way to pray. You'd think the direction of the sun would have been a giveaway, but maybe he figured we'd screwed around with that, too.

It was up to Mark and me to stand in the middle of the cell-block and explain to the detainees in Arabic what was about to take place. We stressed that this was for their own protection and good health and that it wouldn't be painful. They looked confused. Then the lead medic explained step by step what was going to happen. When a medic approached, he told them, each detainee should step forward to the opening in the cell door where food was normally handed in, pull up his shirtsleeve, and place his shoulder against the opening. He would feel a slight pinch as the needle went in, he said, and then it would be over. "If you cooperate, this should be extremely quick and easy," said the medic. I expected otherwise.

As the medics got their supplies ready, the detainees chattered. Some of them looked spooked. A tall, gaunt man who appeared to have some leadership authority said, "Istaed aashaan tikoon shaheed." Be ready to become martyrs. Just as I'd expected.

One of the psych techs asked me what he'd said. "You really want to know?" I replied. A hesitant nod. "They think we're going to kill them," I told him.

Mark and I decided the best strategy was to team up and

try to talk the cellblock leaders into going along with the program. One of them was adamant that we were trying to poison them. "We have been here nearly a year, and we all knew this was coming," he said. "We knew that you would one day make us martyrs."

Another of the detainee leaders seemed more open to us. He just couldn't understand why, if this was supposed to be good for them, we had to force them to take the shot, rather than make it optional. This went on for more than fifteen minutes. The MP cut in. "Let's get this going," he said. "I want you guys off my cellblock before lunch. Explain to these men that they are prisoners of the United States military, not guests at a hotel!"

Mark and I each accompanied a medic, starting at opposite ends of the cellblock. My first two detainees required me to engage in prolonged persuasive dialogue before they stuck out their arms for the injection.

"Move forward, lift your shirtsleeve, and place your arm at the opening," I said in Arabic.

"I don't want to." The first detainee replied.

"This is not going to hurt you. It's a shot to keep you from getting sick. This will actually help you."

"Inta mamloo bilkara," he replied. You are full of shit.

"Honestly, this will not hurt you," I said, annoyed that the whole thing hadn't been handled better. "Every detainee is going to take this," I added, trying to offer him safety in numbers.

"Then why do I have to be first?" he asked.

The medic interrupted. "Tell him this is not an option. If he doesn't move forward now, the MPs will force him to take it and it will be very uncomfortable." The detainee thought for a few seconds and realized we weren't bluffing.

At the behest of my medic, I began telling the rest that this was nonnegotiable. "Either step forward and present your right shoulder for the shot, or the MPs will come into your cell and hold you down for it," I said. I didn't think it would come to that, but it was a possibility.

Mark seemed to have more patience. When I looked down the block to see how he was doing, he was engrossed in explaining that America was not trying to kill everyone at Camp Delta by lethal injection.

Suddenly Mark went to the middle of the cellblock. Speaking loudly in Arabic, he said, "Listen, it is very important for each of you to know that we are *not* trying to kill you. This shot is to protect you from influenza. Since it seems that most of you don't believe us, I am going to prove that the shot will not hurt you." He took off his outer BDU blouse, pulled up the right sleeve of his T-shirt, and the medic stuck the needle in. I had only known Mark three weeks, but this outside-the-box move was right in character.

And it worked. The process started to go more quickly. Eventually we had given the shot to everyone except a dark-skinned British Muslim who was reading the Koran. I gave him the instructions a couple of times: "Move forward and lift your right sleeve." He didn't even look up. Mark came over to see if he could help.

It had been a long morning and we were all ready for lunch. I said, "Listen, you can either take this on your own, or we'll come in there and force you to take it." He looked up from the Koran. "Come on in." We told the guard commander that the Brit seemed intent on being our first genuine holdout. We knew the MPs might call in an IRF. I still hadn't seen one in action.

The guard commander came to talk to the detainee himself. He tried everything in the book. Mo stopped by the cellblock to see if having a native linguist in the mix helped. Not this time.

The commander radioed the IRF team leader and told him to start moving in. Before I saw anything, I heard a detainee in the end cell shout, "Allah al-Akbar." God is great, the common cry when the shit was hitting the fan. Then loud, synchronized stomping as five soldiers entered the block in helmets, over-the-knee shin pads, chest protectors, and thick black-leather gloves. The first soldier in line carried a clear plexiglass shield. They walked in step, each hanging on to the waist of the soldier in front of him. It was like a scene from some storm trooper action film. They were in no rush; the psychological effect of their march down the corridor, boots echoing off the metal floor with frightening, deafening thuds, was powerful. One NCO was following the group with a video camera. I was told the tapes were used for training.

The detainee very slowly kissed his Koran, closed it, placed it in its white covering, and set it on his cell ledge. Then he stood up and took off his orange shirt. He was thin but had a wiry build with sharp muscle definition. We later learned that he'd been a kickboxer at home. The guard commander offered him one last chance. He said nothing and simply indicated he was ready for the IRF team with a wave of his hand.

The air on the block seemed to vibrate as everyone antici- pated the onset of orchestrated violence. Some of the detainees were genuinely frightened, moving to the back of their cells. The others started shouting "American dogs!" "Kafer!" "Allah al-Akbar!" I had never witnessed such mayhem.

The five IRF-team MPs lined up outside the cell door. Start- ing in the back, they each shouted "Ready!" and one by one slapped the shoulder of the next soldier up. The first soldier opened the door and directed a good dose of pepper spray at the detainee, then started to back him into a corner with his shield. But the captive managed to swipe the shield away and tried to kick the second soldier in line. He landed a good blow to the shoulder, but before he could put his foot down the third soldier, thinking fast, grabbed it and jerked. The de- tainee's body rose in the air and came crashing to the metal floor.

All five MPs swarmed over him. One was responsible for se- curing his head, and the other four were supposed to take one limb each. The detainee was kicking and squirming, fueled by his hostility. Mo was shouting to him in Arabic to stop resist- ing. One of the stronger soldiers who had a solid grip on one arm was punching him in the ribs. And through it all, one of the detainee leaders was shouting in Arabic, "They are going to kill him! Allah al-Akbar!"

Then suddenly a female soldier on the team, who was

supposed to be holding down one of the detainee's legs, ran out of the cell and took off her mask, panting. She was clearly not in top physical condition. While she caught her breath, her fellow soldiers struggled to get shackles on the detainee. After about thirty seconds she put her helmet on and went back in. The man was finally pinned down, and the medic came in with his needle and inoculated him.

There was something nonsensical about all this, of course. American soldiers on a tropical island brutally suppressing a man captured in the Global War on Terror—all for the sake of protecting him from the flu.

The guards who had secured the detainee got the job done with minimum trouble. But it was a crapshoot. Every MP at Guantánamo was trained in IRF procedures, and they served on rotating teams, but there were no physical requirements for the job, and it seemed obvious that there should have been. The guard commanders had no idea how much physical training each detainee had, and it was a sure bet that many of these captives dreamed of an opportunity to injure or kill an American. One weak link, like the woman who had stepped out to catch her breath, might be all it would take.

A few days after the flu shot drama, the guard commander stopped by our office to ask if one of us would volunteer to be the "subject" during an IRF training exercise and play the part of an obstreperous detainee. This seemed a little like asking a goldfish to jump into a bowl of paint thinner, given how the guards felt about us. Now they wanted one of us to be their IRF practice dummy, and none of us jumped at the chance. But the guard commander pressed further and said the exercise would take place in the rec yard, rather than a cell. I agreed to give it a try. Mo said he'd done it once before and it wasn't all that bad, and I knew that being in the rec yard would give me room to maneuver and, I hoped, avoid bashing my head on anything metal.

I followed the commander down to the rec yard, with Adam along as the linguist. He gave me the ground rules: I could do anything to try to resist, but if I was in serious pain I was to tell them. I should continue to resist, if I could, once they got me on the ground. The MPs, he said, would use pressure points to try to restrain me. When the team did that effectively, I was to go limp and comply. He asked if I had had any martial arts training, and I told him that my six months of classes in Virginia before arriving in Cuba hadn't made me much of a threat.

"Fight as hard as you can until it hurts," said the commander. "We won't break anything. Ready?"

"Ready as I will be," I said.

He walked behind the cellblock to tell the IRF team to come forward. But while he was gone, one of the other guards beckoned me over. "Hey, Sergeant," he said, "if you can, go after the third guy in the line of live." He said the kid was a jerk and also would be my easiest target physically. I hesitated, but decided that as long as I had volunteered to get the crap beaten out of me by the MPs, I wouldn't go down without a fight.

The IRF team started approaching the rec yard as we played out the training scenario. A guard outside the gate told me, the disgruntled detainee, that my rec time was up. "Go to hell; I'm not coming in," I replied in Arabic. We went through a few rounds of this, then the guard commander showed up and told me that if I didn't comply, they would have to use force. I told him that would be fine. "I'm ready for a fight!" I said. The IRF team, in full regalia, started marching toward me, stopping just outside the fence. I sized them up. The third soldier in line was indeed the smallest, about five foot three and no more than 125 pounds. Maybe I could give these guys a little action before they overwhelmed me.

The five soldiers marched into the rec yard. I started to walk away, but they were surrounding me. I had to make my move. I shuffled to my right and lunged at the pint-sized guy. Another of the soldiers managed to get his arms around my neck, but not before I had mine wrapped around the neck of his teammate. My left arm encircled his helmet and I locked it in place, grabbing my left forearm with my right hand. With my left hand I was reaching under the helmet to unhook his chin strap so I could get my hands around his neck. If I were a terrorist, I was inches away from being able to choke an American soldier. As my fingers were starting to find the strap, I felt someone tackle me. I kept my arms tightly around the neck of the guy I had grabbed and used his body to break my fall.

One member of the IRF team was punching me in the right arm. Two others pinned each of my legs. The fifth soldier had my head and found the pressure points just beneath my ears. I immediately let go of the soldier's neck and went slack. Within thirty seconds I was on my stomach, my ankles were shackled, and my hands were cuffed behind my back.

They put me on a stretcher and two soldiers carried me out while the others held me in place.

We took a few minutes to catch our breath before doing an after-action review. When the officer in charge, a lieutenant, asked the small soldier whom I had almost strangled what went wrong, his only response was "I don't know; it all happened so fast." I didn't say much, but after the dust settled I went to the lieutenant and laid out to him how dangerous the situation could have been. My hands had been about to grab the soldier's chin strap, I stressed, and if I had been a detainee on a mission from God, I just might have been able to get his helmet off. I also noted that the guard responsible for securing my head was outstanding. He found the pressure points quickly and used them effectively. I asked the lieutenant if anyone had considered designating certain soldiers as regular IRF team members. At that point I had no objection to the IRFs; there had to be some way, I thought, for the guards to be able to suppress a detainee who failed to comply with orders or threatened the safety of other inmates. I just thought they should be good at what they did and not endanger our own soldiers.

The lieutenant thanked me for my input and walked away, ignoring my question.

So many of the MPs were inexperienced, either because they were young or they were reservists who hadn't seen much action. I almost felt sorry for them sometimes, getting their trial by fire at a place like Gitmo. Adam, Vanessa, and I were hanging out one quiet afternoon when an urgent-sounding MP called us. Translator needed pronto on cellblock Charlie. It sounded serious, so Adam and I both bolted.

Winding along the gravel through the maze of fencing, we had to go through three of the compound's endless double gates. As we finally cleared into Charlie block, we saw medics rushing there as well, never a good sign. The MP in charge hustled us back to the shower and recreation area. The showers were slapdash contraptions, more like cages than shower stalls, open except for panels placed for modesty's sake. Out in the yard I saw a detainee, blood all over his right arm and covering his feet, being awkwardly hoisted halfway onto a stretcher, the left side of his body dangling off. The space—only about fifteen by twenty yards—was crowded with guards, medics, a doctor, and now two translators.

The doctor was kneeling next to the detainee, and Adam went and knelt next to him. I heard them telling the captive, a Bahraini named Halim, that he was going to be all right. I looked around to see if I could help with anything else. On the ground outside the shower I noticed a pool of dark red blood; the detainee had apparently cut his wrists with a razor. Sitting on the cellblock steps was a trembling national guardsman, a kid of no more than nineteen, trying to calm his nerves with a cigarette.

An MP summoned me over to the shower. There was another puddle of blood, with more smeared on the wall—a river seemed to have spilled from this man's veins. I realized that the blood on the wall was writing: "Intahart min shiddat al-thulm." The senior officer on the scene asked me to translate.

"Sir, it reads: 'I committed suicide because of the brutality of my oppressors,' " I said.

The young soldier cowering on the steps in dusty boots and

a wrinkled shirt had been tasked with monitoring the detainee. When he heard me, he looked horrified. I could see he was blaming himself for the carnage, and I walked over to him.

"This wasn't your fault," I said.

"But I heard what you just said," he replied in a pained voice.

I tried to convince him that the detainee meant "oppressors" writ large, the American infidels, not the guy standing outside his stall, but the kid looked dubious. Green as the grass that was so scarce inside the wire, he had only been at Guantánamo a couple of months. No doubt his day-to-day encounters with the captives were hard enough for him to process, let alone an event like this.

Halim survived, remarkably, and I learned more of his troubled story after the incident. He had arrived within weeks of the opening of Camp X-ray, so had been in detention for almost a year. He'd attended college in Indiana and he spoke English, but he'd barely talked when he first arrived in Gitmo, according to Vanessa, who had met him at X-ray. He always had a dazed look, as if he didn't know where he was. She wondered if he had gone through something terrible at Bagram. Eventually the camp psychologist put the Bahraini on some heavy meds, which gave him his first opportunity to try to kill himself. Halim would fake taking his medication each day and hide the pills in his cell, planning to store up enough so he could take them all at once and end his life. But one of his cellmates ratted him out, and the MPs introduced him to the IRF.

The IRF process was a little more ad hoc then, Vanessa

explained. Getting IRFed at X-ray meant receiving a good old-fashioned ass whipping, after which the lucky detainee would be hogtied—made to kneel with his hands behind his back and his hand and foot shackles locked together—for four hours. Apparently the Red Cross had complained about this to the highest levels of the military command.

Halim didn't speak in the following weeks. He just stared straight ahead. But the day that the MPs were transferring detainees from X-ray to the newly built Camp Delta, Halim received another beating. Vanessa saw him two days after the move and noticed that his face was black and blue. A psych tech told her that he was vastly better than he had been two days earlier. Vanessa tried to investigate why Halim was IRFed the day of the move, but her questions went unanswered. She learned only that there had not been a linguist present and that the MPs had somehow lost the videotape of that particular IRF action.

Soon after Halim got to Camp Delta, he tried another way to end his life. He thought he could scrape enough paint off the cells to eat all at once and do himself in, but it only gave him an upset stomach. Then for a while it appeared that he was starting to make some improvement—until the day he requested a razor in the shower, supposedly to shave his body hair. It seemed insane to me that a detainee who had twice previously tried to kill himself would be allowed to take a razor into the shower. But at this point, things not making sense at the camp was starting to become the norm.

Throughout that day, I found myself more numb than upset about the incident. I was mostly baffled that some MP, maybe the kid, had made the attempt so easy by giving Halim a razor, probably just through carelessness. But when I lay down at night, I found myself staring at the ceiling, thinking about whether Halim's family knew where he was. I wondered if he had helped Al Qaeda or the Taliban, or if other circumstances had brought him to Gitmo. And I wondered if we really had anything on him.

The mental health personnel and the guards always had to be on the watch for detainees who might try to harm themselves. The psych techs' rounds were rarely helpful in this regard. Occasionally we would get word through the leadership channels that a mass suicide was planned; a detainee had told his interrogator about it. Once we heard they were going to try to stab themselves in the ears with sharpened tools made from the plastic spoons in their MREs, which sounded like something from a Monty Python skit. But the camp personnel had to take it seriously.

Even with all that awareness of the danger, suicide attempts were much too frequent. I was off duty one day when the quiet Mormon on our team, Paul, was talking to a Saudi detainee who'd been spending a lot of time in interrogations recently. He claimed he was a schoolteacher and had no involvement with Al Qaeda. The other captives on his cellblock were convinced he had turned and was coughing up information. They had been telling him for days that he was a traitor, that he would go to hell. "You have betrayed your faith!" they would say. "You will burn in hell! Why are you working with them? You should go ahead and kill yourself." They intentionally kept him up at night with their taunts and accusations, imposing their own kind of sleep deprivation. He asked to go into solitary, but his fellow captives still banged on the walls and yelled at him.

On this day, he said to Paul, "If you don't get me a room where there's nobody else around, I'm going to kill myself." Paul told the guards, who didn't show much concern and said they had no authority to separate him. The Saudi said, "No, you don't understand, if I don't get out of here in half an hour, I'm going to kill myself." Paul went to talk to the MPs' NCOIC for the day, who in turn said a move was impossible because the intelligence side hadn't okayed it. By the time Paul went back to deliver the bad news, the Saudi was swinging from a noose he'd fashioned from strips of bedsheet. Paul rushed to find an MP and they cut him down. A doctor quicky arrived to perform CPR, but it was unclear how long the man had been hanging and serious damage already had been done.

The detainee was in a coma for months. It didn't get out to the press for a while. In fact, we used to talk in the office about how the number of suicide attempts being reported in the news seemed to be far too low. We could never make the numbers match up.

CHAPTER FIVE

In my first month at Gitmo, I both loved and hated what I
was doing. On the plus side, I knew I was gaining a lot of
valuable experience for future intel assignments. My Arabic
was getting better fast, thanks in part to the detainees themselves. I'd found that although my vocabulary wasn't bad, I
sometimes mangled pronunciations so horribly that they had
no idea what I was saying. They coached me through it. I'd
learned some new expressions from them too, such as the
word for traitor—*khaen*—their favorite epithet for the Muslim linguists and those among them they thought were
spilling in interrogation. That one hadn't come up in my work
prior to this.

I'd started to hate the work for some of the same reasons. I
found that my understanding of Islam and Arabic culture was
deepening as I heard more and more of the detainees' stories.
Some of the linguists still barely talked to the detainees, and a

couple of them showed outright contempt for them, but most of us had conversations with them fairly regularly. I was feeling all the more strongly that simply walling yourself off from them made no sense, either for me personally or for the whole operation.

But the troubling part of talking with the detainees and getting more familiar with their views, both of Americans and of Islam, and seeing the depth of their commitment to their religion was that it made me a good deal more aware of just how badly we misunderstood each other. Mustapha, who called me over whenever I was on Echo block, drove this home to me more than anyone else.

One morning he said to me, "I've been thinking about our conversations. I have some more questions for you."

"What's on your mind, Mustapha?"

"You say that America is a religious country, that people's faith is important to them."

"Yes, that's true," I said.

"I never heard that. I thought all Americans were atheists." He said, "I'm not sure I believe you."

"We have many different faiths, and there are some atheists," I said, "but there's no doubt religion has a very powerful influence on our culture. Our money even says In God We Trust. We're definitely a country full of believers."

He paused, contemplating a bit, then asked, "Do you believe evil exists?"

"Yes, I do, Mustapha. Do you?"

"Taban," he replied. Of course.

"Mustapha," I asked, "is the justification for jihad that you're fighting evil?"

"That is exactly what jihad is about."

"Well, who decides what evil is?" I asked.

"Allah says what is evil." He answered, perplexed.

"And how do you know what Allah thinks is evil? Through the Koran?" I asked.

"Of course, but sometimes a good Muslim just knows when something is evil."

"I think most Christians feel the same way; we know what evil is. To us, terrorism is evil. Al Qaeda is evil. The jihad you're fighting is evil."

"That is only because you don't understand," he said.

"You're right, Mustapha; I don't understand that kind of hate."

In the linguists' office we often talked about the detainees and their religion, discussing whether we thought they were brainwashed or just passionate about their faith. The general consensus was that it depended on the detainee; some were brainwashed, others were just fervent. And some seemed to have lost faith altogether. They were often the ones who tried to kill themselves.

I was starting to wonder whether our war on terror would be counterproductive. I'd seen how Camp Delta was breaking down the will—and the will to live—of some of the detainees, but I'd also seen how for others it seemed only to have strengthened their resolve and their solidarity against their American oppressors. From what I'd seen so far at Gitmo, I had to question how effectively we were isolating the actual evildoers.

None of us outside of JIG were in a position to know how much valuable intel was being spilled by the captives, but I'd heard rumors that very little good information was coming from most of them. One afternoon at lunch I ran into two linguists on the JIG team and told them I hoped they were getting the goods on Al Qaeda. "Maybe in the interrogations I'm not in," one of them said drily. And, of course, there was the issue that so many of the detainees weren't going into interrogation at all anymore.

Meanwhile, I'd heard one story after another from the detainees about how they'd ended up at the camp, and I couldn't help but find some of them troubling. With each story I heard, each detainee I got to know, I found it a little harder to accept that the policy of never formally charging them with their crimes was a necessary evil in the war on terror. It's a lot easier to justify a policy when you don't have to see those who are locked away up close and hear about their families and backgrounds. Frankly, Vanessa's suggestion about shutting off my feelings sometimes seemed an enviable option. But I didn't have a clue how to do it even if I wanted to.

In the army we weren't trained to give much attention to our feelings, or even to critical thinking. It was assumed that situations would be more or less black and white. It was a privilege to wear the uniform of the American military and fight for your country. You put it on, conducted your assigned mission, and went home. Guantánamo, however, was the land of ambiguity, a landscape in shades of gray. Any thinking individual had to be influenced by the paradoxes all around us. If you weren't, you were in a mental fog.

*   *   *

Aziz was a Saudi who'd been picked up by the Northern Alliance in Afghanistan. He was a short pudgy man with a gray beard and shaggy salt-and-pepper hair who appeared to be in his forties, and he made us laugh almost every day. He would tell me jokes in Arabic that I didn't get, and talk about how much he hated that women wore the burka in Afghanistan. He'd say he wished he lived in the States so he could see women's bodies, and he'd regularly hit on some of the female guards and linguists, especially Vanessa, calling her *imra al-ahlam*, "girl of my dreams." One day when I went to his cell, it was clear that he had called for a translator simply hoping to shoot the shit. He complained about the guards and claimed that they treated the entire cellblock disrespectfully. I told him that I had no control over that. Then he started asking me questions.

"What is the army like, Basam?"

"I like it Aziz; I love serving my country. The army taught me Arabic, and I get to travel a lot."

"Why does your country always support Israel?" he said.

"Aziz, you know I can't talk about things like that."

"I know; I just was hoping we could debate a bit."

"No debates today, Aziz."

"Taib," he said. OK.

"Ya Basam, I noticed you have no wedding ring; you are a bachelor, yes?"

"For now I am, Aziz, but hopefully not much longer. I plan to get married soon."

"Does that mean that while you are here you can have sex with any of the women on the base?" Aziz asked with a completely straight face.

I laughed and said, "What would make you think that, Aziz?"

"Look, Basam, I'm not a fool; there is no way these women in uniforms are really here as soldiers. Do you think we are stupid? All of the detainees know the truth—that they are here to service the real soldiers."

I couldn't believe what I was hearing. "No, Aziz, the women that are on the base are equal soldiers with the men." Aziz started to laugh hysterically.

"Basam," Aziz said when he'd stopped laughing, "someday I hope we can have an honest conversation and you can stop feeding me this shit. Do you actually expect me to believe that the girl with long blond hair and great big breasts is a *soldier*?"

"She is, Aziz, and she is a damn good one." I had to get myself out of this conversation.

I started to walk away, but Aziz could see me smiling.

"You know I'm right!" He yelled as I walked away.

But when Aziz wasn't joking and making fun of the detainees around him, he was in the corner of his cell crying. Like Wael, he claimed he'd been picked up by the Northern Alliance for a bounty simply because he was an Arab in Afghanistan. He told me he missed his grandchildren. "I don't want to die in jail," he pleaded. He said he used to love America.

The fact that some of our captives had no business being at Guantánamo was plain to anyone who paid a visit to Delta block. One day, right around lunchtime, a call from Delta came in. Nobody wanted to take it and risk running late to meet Rosco for the run to the main base dining facility. Missing the van meant you were stuck eating another second-rate meal in the camp mess tent. I was still trying to make a good impression and besides, I'd never been to Delta, so I volunteered to go. The others chortled as I went out the door, and Vanessa teased me, "Have fun!"

As I entered the block, from one of the first cells I passed came a hiss: "Whaasssssssuuuuuuup?" I did a double take. Where would this Muslim captive have heard the Budweiser ad? He cracked me up, but I tried not to show it.

I found the detainee with the complaint. "The librarian hates me and deliberately skips me when he delivers books." Highly unlikely, but I told him I'd look into it and get back to him. As I started to walk away, another detainee called, "Mutarjim, mutarjim." Then in English, he said, "I want to tell you something." I figured, why not see what this guy wants? When I approached, he said in Arabic, "I know a little English; I want you to tell me if it is good." "Let me hear it," I said.

And then this Arab, a suspect in the Global War on Terror who was locked away behind green steel mesh, got up from his cross-legged position on the floor, looked me in the eye, and started to rap: "I like big butts and I cannot lie, you other brothers can't deny, that when a girl walks in with an itty-bitty waist . . ." With perfect locution and rhythm, he serenaded me with the chorus of Sir Mix-A-Lot's raunchy eighties classic "I Like Big Butts." I didn't know if I should laugh or cry. These guys definitely had a different sort of spark.

Over time, I realized that some of the men on Delta block were truly mentally disturbed. The detainees there were not only those who were considered the most depressed and at highest risk of attempting suicide; some of them were just flat out crazy and belonged in a mental institution. I heard that one former Delta resident used to eat his own feces, and that he'd been sent home before I arrived on the island. Were these men unbalanced before they got to Gitmo, easy pickings for warlords hunting bounties? Or was it Camp Delta, with its endless uncertainty, that pushed them over the edge?

Some of the other detainees could have been having delusions, but it was impossible to tell fact from fiction. During my fifth week or so I was translating for a detainee on Foxtrot block who wanted to see a doctor about an ingrown toenail. I told him I would tell the MPs to put it in their notebook. He said, "Make sure they write it in, Basam."

"Mish mooshkila," I said. No problem.

As I started to walk down the corridor to go speak with the MP, another detainee got my attention.

"What's up?" I said to him in Arabic. He was white, with reddish hair, and he turned out to be one of the camp's Chechnyans.

"Do you know the status of my briefcase?" he said.

I had no idea what he was talking about and thought I might be misunderstanding his Arabic. "What?" I asked, puzzled.

"My briefcase, do you know where it is?"

At this point I was pretty confident I understood, but asked for clarification anyway.

"Are you asking me about a briefcase?" I asked.

"Yes, I am. Surely you know about my situation and the briefcase I had when I arrived."

"Actually, I have no idea what you are talking about, and I've never heard of your briefcase."

The detainee sighed, appearing exasperated. "When I was apprehended in Chechnya, I was carrying a black briefcase filled with cash," he said. "Upon my arrival here, my interrogator assured me that he would find out about it and let me know the status of the briefcase and what would happen to the cash. Two weeks later I saw a new interrogator, and he told me he knew nothing of my briefcase. After a month of interrogations I finally got that interrogator to agree to check into the issue, and he said he would then let me know the status of the briefcase. I heard nothing from him for four weeks. Then, the next time I went, my new interrogator of course knew nothing of the briefcase. I have also discussed this with the blond girl, and she, too, told me she would check into the issue."

As I listened I almost wanted to laugh, but I knew that I couldn't do that.

He had a look of total indignation. "I know that those American dogs are spending all my money! I just want to know if I'm getting any of it back or if I can send it back to my family."

"I really will have to ask about this," I said. "But to be honest with you, I'm not too important around here; I doubt anyone will give me any answers."

"I would appreciate it if you would just ask," he said kindly.

"No problem. I'll let you know if I find out anything."

When I returned to the office, Vanessa and Mo were there reading magazines. I closed the door and said, "Do either of you know about some guy who was asking about a briefcase filled with money?"

They just looked at each other and had a good laugh. Apparently, this guy had the same conversation with every linguist every time he or she walked by his cell.

Some of my teammates had begun to question the mission of the camp in large part because of stories like the one Aziz had told me. They were convinced that few of the detainees had any real intelligence value, and had doubts about the guilt of a large part of the camp's population. The number of detainees who hardly came across as terrorists had definitely started to eat at me. I'd learned we were holding a group of Afghani teenagers who ranged from about twelve to fourteen years old and were kept in a separate facility called Camp Iguana. Iguana was a former officer's cottage, outside the wire, with a real view of the ocean. The kids, who were now being tutored in various school subjects, had more freedom than our detainees, but they couldn't leave the yard of their fenced-in holding area. Still, I had to wonder about the wisdom of keeping kids so young in a place like Gitmo.

It wasn't just the observant Muslims who were dubious, but they were more open about it, just as Ahmad had been with Mark and me on our first day in the camp. They'd also started distancing themselves from the rest of us, and it seemed to me they fed on one another's grievances. They prayed together daily and had Friday Koranic study meetings, and they also socialized together. It wasn't unusual for Captain Mansur and Ahmad to spend a day off doing some boating. Fraternization between officers and enlisted men was generally off-limits in the service, but most of us were happy enough to overlook it in the strange circumstances we were in—unless it seemed to be leading to favoritism as well. To some on the team, that line had been crossed, and the fact that the tie of Islam was trumping normal military decorum was starting to rub some of us the wrong way.

I thought again about the weird blend of ethnicities and religious beliefs among the members of our group, most of them brought to Camp Delta only out of expediency, because they spoke a required language. Besides the committed Muslims, there was Elena, the Russian linguist, ethnic Jew, and atheist; Leema, an Arabic linguist who was a Lebanese American moderate Muslim army reservist; and Pops, a Palestinian Christian who'd emigrated to the United States and become an army reserve mechanic. Staff Sergeant Alan Beaumonde, the laid-back, always upbeat Haitian NCOIC of our group, didn't subscribe to any organized religion that we could tell. We had a Mormon, Paul; several practicing Christians, including Mark, who was born again; and a few Muslims who had a fairly secular outlook, like Mo. For many in the group, religion wasn't a big deal, but for others it was a lodestar, and although some would say they didn't care much about politics or about what was going on at the camp, others were carrying a good deal of baggage.

Mo would say he had no problem with the camp; he was just there to do his job and get out, a marine through and through. Marines just stir up shit, the saying goes, they don't worry about where it lands. Once he said to me, "I really wonder if that guy on Echo block is innocent. He says so every day, and I think I'm starting to believe him." But for the most part, Mo was more concerned about trying to get laid, which became his all-consuming mission once he started to think he might have to go to Iraq when he left Gitmo.

Then there was Len. He was an army reservist from Southern California, but his family was Chaldean Christian, from Iraq. They hadn't been treated well by Saddam's regime, and I think he saw Gitmo as a chance to exact some revenge against Muslims. For the most part, Len was a hell of a nice guy, and the kind you'd undoubtedly want next to you in a foxhole. I had no question that in the line of fire, he would have your back.

He was an aspiring actor—he'd had some bit parts in movies and TV—and an avid weight lifter, and his body was covered with tattoos. He did everything with passion. When he lifted, he was the guy you heard grunting all the way across the gym; his arms were the size of car tires from his nightly workouts. When he laughed, he held nothing back. It was loud, mouth-wide-open roaring. In conversation you were the center of his attention; he was 100 percent engrossed. And when he was pissed, you wanted to be a couple of mountain ranges away.

With Len, you always knew exactly where he stood, and he had no qualms about letting you know what he thought about the camp. He said he wished we could torture the captives and that he'd gladly accept the role of torturer in chief.

I'd figured from the start that if our team was to be successful, we would have to be highly sensitive to one another's differences. But Captain Mansur, who had never been in command of any unit before, let alone anything like our strange brew, exercised little control over the growing tensions. Our chemistry had grown more volatile by the week.

Things had really heated up right around Christmas, when Mo said he'd heard from Captain Mansur that there was an air-bridge mission coming up. These were round-trip flights from Gitmo to Afghanistan to pick up captured terrorist suspects of high enough interest to send on to our neck of the ocean. The trips required some of us to go along, depending on what languages the captives spoke. This particular journey called for one Arabic and one Pashto translator.

All of us wanted in on it. It meant action. It meant going to a combat zone. Of course, there were times when trapping land crabs in the beastly noonday sun would have been a welcome change from sitting in our cramped trailer office waiting for calls to translate a detainee's complaint about how the guards had crushed his lunchtime cookies again.

Mo had heard a lot about these trips, and he said they were extremely intense. "Every single aspect of the mission is meant to intimidate the detainees," he told me. "Even the linguists are supposed to treat the detainees like shit and get them scared out of their minds." Not long before my arrival, an air force linguist who had gone on one of the missions took photos, which found their way onto television. The bound captives wore dark goggles, headphones, and paper masks like those used by health care workers. During portions of the transfer they were hooded, and they were laced down to the floor of the C-130 with black straps for the more than twenty-hour flight. Some thought they were being sent to their deaths, and nobody disabused them of that notion. They were screamed at constantly during the trip. On the ground in Cuba, they were immediately thrown into interrogation booths for sessions that could last up to two days. I heard that these grillings often produced more information than months of subsequent questioning.

But paradoxically, the Arabic linguist chosen for this trip was Ahmad, who had openly said he wanted to avoid interacting with the detainees because he found himself identifying with them too much. If intimidation of the suspects was one of the goals, Mansur had picked the wrong guy for the job. Not only that, but there were a number of more senior linguists who deserved the assignment, we thought, like Pops. Captain Mansur hadn't consulted with our NCOIC, Sergeant Beaumonde, which would be the normal procedure; the NCOIC is the hands-on unit leader, the one responsible for training, disciplining, and rewarding its members.

Apparently, Ahmad wanted to go out of curiosity, to see how things were done. Still, some of the non-Muslim linguists complained that Captain Mansur was favoring a fellow devout Muslim. The objection to favoritism was being aired more and more often and openly, and this seemed a glaring case.

Then, a few days before New Year's, Captain Mansur banned Len from having any contact with the detainees. Len had come back to the office fuming after taking a call. He could barely tell the story between outbursts of "I hate these terrorist motherfuckers." He said he'd just talked to a detainee who was upset because he hadn't gotten his medicine that day. Len said he'd relay the complaint to the MPs. "No," the detainee shouted. "I need you to help me yourself. The guards don't care."

Len said his job was only to translate, and then he added, "And furthermore, I don't care either!" The detainee spewed an increasingly vehement litany of insults at Len, impugning his family, calling him a Kafer—infidel—and an "American dog." Then he topped it all off by spitting in Len's face. The detainee was lucky to have steel between him and Len. First, Len spit back at him and told him he wanted to get in his cell and break his neck. Then he shouted every Arabic epithet he knew at the top of his lungs.

Len's yelling and rattling the cell door provoked all the other detainees on the block to begin shouting in solidarity with Len's nemesis. "Allah al-Akbar" chants spread from that block to three others nearby—nearly two hundred riled-up detainees united against their American captors all because one linguist couldn't control his temper. The NCOIC on the block had to try to calm Len down and asked him to leave.

That night Len retold the story while a few of us were eating kebabs at 19A, and Ahmad grew furious. "Why would you react in such a way, Len?"

"What the fuck are you talking about, Ahmad?" Len replied, drinking his beer.

"I mean, why would you get so frustrated with this guy? Why not just help him and walk away?"

"Why do you feel so sorry for these bastards, Ahmad?"

"I don't necessarily feel sorry for them. But I do think we should treat them respectfully. None of them have been tried for anything yet, don't forget."

"Trials my ass!" Len shouted. "We should take them all out on a boat with six hundred fucking anchors and send them to the bottom of the ocean. Problem solved. We could all leave this place." We had heard this before from Len, who always said he wished he could convey his endgame to General Miller, the two-star in charge of the detainee operation.

Ahmad walked away in disgust.

Captain Mansur finally decided to respond to all the grumbling he'd heard about the air-bridge mission. He scheduled a meeting at 19A on New Year's Eve at 2000. Predictably enough, this was hugely popular with the drinking members of the team, which meant just about everyone except the devout Muslim group. Most of us figured it was his intention to deter the "infidels" among us from having a few brewskies to ring in the New Year.

By 2015 Captain Mansur was still nowhere to be found, and some of the natives were starting to get restless. "Were you guys planning to drink tonight?" Dan asked Mo and me. Definitely. "Well, let's get started," he said, although clearly he already had. He walked over to the cooler and popped a beer.

We hung on till around 2100, then dug into the cooler. Finally, Captain Mansur arrived and made no excuses. "I called this meeting to clear up some issues that I've heard talk about on this team," he said. "First, regarding the air-bridge mission, I am sending Ahmad as the Arabic linguist and Staff Sergeant Tessler as the Pashto linguist. The decision has been made and it's final."

What followed was the most confrontational exchange I'd ever witnessed between a group of enlisted men and their commanding officer. Captain Mansur was clearly defensive, and he let the meeting go on much too long. All the while, the practicing Muslims didn't say a word. In my prior experience, any OIC would have let us know in no uncertain terms that debate was over: "This issue is closed; if I hear anyone complaining about this again, you'll have my boot up your ass." That kind of response generally worked quite well in the army.

At one point Captain Mansur mentioned that he'd never been in command of service members before. All I could think was that it certainly showed. I kept my mouth shut, which was unusual for me when opinions were flying, but I was too much the straitlaced soldier to jump into the mess. Mostly I was shocked by the unmilitary melee, though on some level I was also simply fascinated. This would definitely spice things up on the job over the next few months.

Gitmo was turning out to be one of those once-in-a-lifetime, far-from-home, pressure-cooker experiences that can forge a lasting camaraderie among those going through it together. Instead, my unit was blowing apart. Some of us stuck around a while that night, had more beers, and bitched.

"Why the hell couldn't we have done that at 1800?" Turk said. "Mo, you do realize it's nearly midnight and all the girls at the Windjammer have already decided who they're sleeping with tonight. Looks like you're ringing in the new year alone."

"Fuck you, Turk," Mo shot back.

Turk raised his beer in acknowledgment.

"You know, my friends," Dan said, "Captain Mansur actually thinks we are all fucking infidels destined for hell."

My first reaction was that that was the alcohol talking, but then I thought again. There we were, five guys—Turk, Mo, Rambo, Dan, and me—pounding beers, working hard to have no less than a nice buzz going by the time the year 2003 rolled around, and I realized Dan was right. To our commander, we were infidels.

I went home and tried to call Darcie at midnight. But I wasn't the only one with that idea, and the base phone system, the fucking monopoly that dug fifty-three cents from our pockets for every minute we spent talking to someone back home, couldn't handle the traffic. All the lines were busy. I finally got through at 12:15. But as usual, I could say very little to her about what was going on at the camp.

When I volunteered, I had a vision of what I thought Gitmo should be, what I had expected it to be: a well-oiled, smartly run facility where our best intelligence personnel sucked information out of the worst terrorists we had captured so we could turn around and capture even worse ones, keeping American shores safe. Yet that picture wasn't matching up with what I was seeing. I knew part of my disillusionment had to do with the fact that I wasn't working on the intelligence side, as I had expected to do. But the festering animosities on our team made it harder to do even the Mickey Mouse assignment I did have. And from my perspective, the signals that something wasn't right—the reports of bounties paid, the captives who weren't being questioned—were just too glaring to ignore.

CHAPTER SIX

One afternoon in mid-January, Adam returned from a call and asked Vanessa, "Do we have any updates on the status of the guys who were sent home a few months ago? One of the detainees was asking about them. He wanted to know if he'd be leaving soon too. Do we even know where they went?"

"I think they returned to Afghanistan," Vanessa replied.

"What are you guys talking about?" I interjected. I was stunned. "Have we already sent some detainees home? Why would we have done that?"

Vanessa explained that four men, two of them at least in their seventies, had been sent back in October.

"Basically," Vanessa continued, "it means that they should never have been sent here in the first place. They never raised a weapon against us, and we don't believe they ever intend to." Backing that up, Vanessa said she had recently chatted with a few interrogators who said the JIG list of detainees who never should have set foot in Gitmo was nearing one hundred. Interrogators weren't supposed to discuss what was going on in the JIG operation, so if they'd spilled this scoop to her, they must not have considered it news anymore.

This was a jolt. The logical conclusion was that either we had sent, and were going to send, terrorists back to plot further attacks against us—and it wasn't likely that the intel side would be so far off on that score—or we really had been holding, for many months, men who were wrongly apprehended. I wasn't naive. I understood that in the fog of war, innocent noncombatants occasionally get picked up. But I had a hard time understanding why my country's leadership would send them to Cuba, refuse to present them with specific charges, and trap them in a legal no-man's-land.

We still were holding some men who doubtless met the age requirement for Social Security. One afternoon, Mo and I were at the medical clinic translating for an elderly Yemeni detainee who complained of chest pains. As the doctor examined him, the patient told him he had been scheduled to have heart surgery back home.

The medical staff was always in a tough spot when it came to detainee health care. They were lied to on a regular basis by captives complaining of phantom conditions. But the doctor believed this man had had a mild heart attack in the morning, and said he would advise the guards of his condition and get him moved to the cellblock closest to the clinic. The guards would be told that if the captive had more chest pains, he should be sent immediately to the clinic for an EKG.

The Yemeni kept saying he was innocent and had no idea

why he was being detained. "Did the Americans send me here to die?" he asked. He was worried he would pass away without being able to say good-bye to his family. When Mo and I got back to our office, I asked him, "Why do you think we have a guy here who may be in his seventies?" Mo suggested I not worry about it.

I kept telling myself the man was just trying to manipulate us, as so many of the detainees did. I knew it was possible he'd been running a safe house or engaged in some other activity that helped Al Qaeda. But what if he hadn't? What if someone gave the United States bogus information because they had a grudge over a donkey deal gone bad with this guy? That night Mark, like Mo, tried to get me to move on. "Erik," he said after we'd talked over a few bottles of Miller Lite, "anybody with any brains around here knows that we've got at least a few people who are innocent, just by virtue of how they were apprehended. You can't allow yourself to think about crap like that or this will be a long assignment. Better to have a few innocent guys here than a bunch of terrorists wandering the hills of Afghanistan."

A few hours after I got to work the next day I received a request for a translator at the medical clinic. I grabbed Mo, who was returning from another call, because I didn't yet feel completely comfortable translating in emergency medical situations.

The same elderly man from the previous day was curled up on the table moaning loudly and complaining of chest pains. The physician's assistant treating him was the skeptical type when it came to detainees' complaints. She told Mo to tell the patient they had checked his vital signs and he should be fine. Mo relayed the message, but the man was shouting in Arabic that he was having a heart attack. Impatiently, the physician's assistant said, "Tell him he is not having a heart attack and he'll be fine." Mo asked her if the doctor from the day before was around. She barked back, "No, he is not here, and we no longer need your help. The patient will be fine without you."

Mo tried to explain that the doctor had wanted to perform an EKG when the detainee was feeling the chest pains he'd experienced yesterday. "The patient will be okay," she insisted, and ripped Mo a new one for telling her how to do her job.

Just as we were leaving, the doctor from the day before walked in, saw the man on the table, and immediately asked if an EKG had been done, as he had requested in his notes. The lower-ranking navy woman had indeed screwed up.

A few days later, Captain Mansur gave us the word about a new camp greeting we were all supposed to start using. The lower-ranking soldier was supposed to say "Honor bound" and salute the higher up, who was supposed to respond "To defend freedom," and return the salute. Most people started doing it. I never once did. I just kept saying "Good morning." I had started to feel like the place wasn't all that honorable. Mark didn't do it because he thought it was bullshit.

Meanwhile, the fractures in the linguist group weren't getting any better. Mo and Ahmad, who lived in the same house, were barely speaking anymore. Mo told Mark and me that one night he and Rambo went out to the Windjammer and struck up a conversation with a couple of air force women. Mo invited one of them back to his place, where Ahmad slept in the kitchen because the house had more tenants than beds. Ahmad was reading on his mattress while Mo and the woman watched TV. Finally, Mo turned off the set and started to head upstairs with his new friend. Ahmad yelled to Mo in Arabic, "Iltaq Allah." Fear God. Mo was no hothead, but Ahmad was lucky there was a lady in the house.

Every new incident with the team drove home how starkly different this assignment was from the usual military undertaking. It was a challenge to relax amid the mounting stress. Our friendly MP housemates, with whom we'd bonded so closely from our first day on base, had moved out, which was a help, but they were replaced within a week by a crew of marine cooks. You might think this would be a gastronomic advantage, leading to reduced consumption of frozen dinners and Hot Pockets in the household. Sadly, that was not the case. Most of these guys, who had been called up from the reserves, were trained to do little more than heat up preprepared meals. And, like their predecessors, they were slobs, although less hostile ones. We had no more in common with them than we had had with the MPs they replaced.

Mark, after weeks of nagging, finally got me to go snorkeling with him one day. We were surrounded by the ocean, but not enjoying it nearly enough. I went to the pool near us a lot, and Mark and I had recently found another one that was a little haven of fun. It had a kick-ass water slide with a twirl in the middle. We spent the day lining up for it, the only alleged adults among the throng of kids twelve and under.

The pool was a strange reminder that "normal" life was happening all around us. Navy and other military personnel who had nothing to do with the detention camp and were stationed at the base for the usual two to three years brought their families along. Moms and dads were sending their children to school, shopping for groceries, going to McDonald's, renting movies, and bowling—in other words, living oddly standard American suburban lives. When we left the camp and went to the pool, we were moving in and out of two completely separate worlds. The world where I threw myself down the pool slide with the eight-year-olds was undoubtedly the better one.

But Mark was bored with the pool and insisted it was time to see some fish, so one Saturday we rented snorkeling gear and headed for the spot on the island that was reported to have the best diving. We jumped off the dock and Mark immediately headed for deep water. I followed, and before we knew it, we were a good distance from the shore and somewhat at the mercy of the strong ocean current.

Each time we dove down we found stuff I'd never seen before—brilliant patches of color with fins, big turtles that moved like principal dancers in the Joffrey compared to how they lumbered on land. I stuck with Mark, occasionally veering off to see something amazing. He apparently had some goal in mind. I finally stopped him perhaps a mile from where we'd started. Our view of the shore was blocked by a huge rock formation that jutted straight down into the water. I asked Mark where the fuck we were going.

"On a little adventure," he replied.

"We've already been carried away by the current and we might need a boat to get us back. Where the hell are you taking me?"

"Right there." He pointed toward the rock formation.

I noticed that the water seemed a bit restless there. "Are you fucking nuts? Why do you want to go in there?"

"Because it will be interesting, Erik. Don't be such a pussy. There's a little cave in there one of the MPs told me about last week. He said it's pretty awesome." He saw the look on my face. "It'll be harmless. I promise we'll get out of there unscathed."

I don't know if I was persuaded or shamed into it, but I followed him. The current seemed stronger. We paused about twenty yards from our destination. "Here's the deal," Mark said. "Supposedly there's some pretty cool stuff right underneath that area over there, in some caves."

"Caves?" I said. "They'll be dark. How the hell will we see anything? And how will we know where they end?"

"If you can't hold your breath any longer, just turn around and leave. We're good swimmers. You'll be able to find your way out, don't worry."

I knew this was a dumb thing to be doing, but I was also curious. As we approached the underwater rocks, there was no sunlight whatsoever. We could barely see where we were going. I followed Mark, who appeared to be trusting his instincts. Finally, we came to an opening that obviously went into a cave. We swam in, and couldn't see a thing. I could barely make out Mark's bright yellow fins in front of me. Was this some MP's idea of a joke? Would we hit a wall, or was there a back way out? My lungs starting to strain, I tapped Mark's leg and pointed backward. Reverse course; chalk it up to a mistake. Mark wanted to go on, fuck the consequences. I figured I'd follow him just a little farther to see if any light appeared.

Sure enough, we came to an opening, but it was narrow. Mark made it through all right. Being about forty pounds heavier, though, I scraped my back across a rock as I swam out. Then, before we surfaced, a wave caught me and my left shoulder banged into another rock. At last I got to the surface and gasped for air.

We were still trying to catch our breath when Mark said, "That was fucking awesome!"

"That," I answered, feeling like shark bait as my scratches bled into the water, "was fucking stupid!"

The next time I ventured into the ocean with Mark it was for above-the-surface sports. In late January a small group of us got together to go waterskiing. A fairly new member of the team named Jake, who was a quiet airman and worked in DO-CEX, came along, as well as Leema and Elena, the Russian-born MP who, I'd come to find, was much friendlier than she'd seemed on first impression. We drove over to the marina near the NEX. While Jake and Mark walked over to reserve the boat and equipment, a woman I recognized from DLI came toward me. I hadn't known Lisa was at Gitmo; she was assigned to JIG, the intelligence unit.

After we caught up on where mutual acquaintances had scattered around the world, she asked me what I was doing and what I thought of the place. I told her I was a little disappointed with the work on JDOG and that my team had serious problems. "I can't complain about the hours," I said, "but I certainly don't think I'm saving the world." She said she'd heard about the bad vibes in our group.

Lisa had been at the camp for a year and had a good handle

on what was going on. She seemed to have had her hand in every pot; when she first arrived, she'd worked the blocks but had then transferred to JIG. Now she supervised more than thirty civilian linguists assigned to the JIG team in an intelligence-producing office she couldn't discuss then and there, and also participated in interrogations.

I did hear loud and clear from her that she loved her boss and her job. And then she mentioned that she was looking for someone to take her place; she was scheduled to leave in a few weeks. I hoped she wouldn't notice my drooling.

That job would get me off the blocks and into some nitty-gritty intel work at last. It would also get me away from my squabbling team, though things had gotten so bad that the most pissed-off people weren't actually speaking much to one another anymore. Ahmad, who had been promised a deployment of just ninety days and had asked to go home even sooner, had just been told his tour was being indefinitely extended, and he had sunk into a deep funk. To make matters even worse for him, Captain Mansur had just made him camp librarian, a position that would put him in contact with the detainees every day. The librarian was everyone's best friend. If this wasn't a guarantee that Ahmad would become an emotional wreck, further affecting our team, I didn't know what was. Just another example of Captain Mansur's brilliant leadership skills. I'd come to see the JDOG operation as undisciplined, unmilitary, and unprofessional. Lisa's job was clearly a whole different ball game.

As I'd heard and seen a growing list of troubling things about the camp, I had become increasingly unhappy that I wasn't getting any insights from the intel side. The thing I'd most loved about intel work was that it gave you a look at the big picture, including aspects of our national defense and foreign policy strategies that were frequently hidden from view, knowledge that filled in many of the blanks that the public was sometimes disturbed about. That was what had motivated me to come to Gitmo. Translating for detainees complaining about backaches just didn't appeal on the same level. I told Lisa I'd like to be considered for the slot.

She led me near a docked pontoon boat and introduced me to her boss, Major Beth Richards, who was in charge of all military and civilian linguists assigned to JIG and who happened to be opening a Budweiser. Lisa was an E-4, one level below my rank of sergeant E-5, and yet here she was socializing with a major. Just the notion of an E-4 spending the day partying, with alcohol, with her boss was astonishing, further evidence that a lot of the normal military rules didn't apply at Gitmo. I told Major Richards that I'd like to be considered for Lisa's job, and she seemed interested. She said they'd be in touch soon. I knew that those on my team who had backgrounds in intel would have killed for this opportunity, including Mark, but then they didn't know about it.

I felt hopeful when the others came back and we took off in our speedboat. We went out a good distance, taking turns on the skis. After we'd been on the water about an hour and it was my turn, we spotted some guys on a pontoon boat whom we had seen earlier on the dock. We didn't know them, but they were MPs. Given the general tenor of our interactions with their species so far, we couldn't resist having a little fun.

"How good are you on those things, Erik?" Tony asked me.

"I don't know. I'm okay, I guess. Why?"

Tony steered the boat within spitting distance of the MPs and I skied by, irrigating them with good spray of the Caribbean as I cut into a turn. Sophomoric, but greatly satisfying—much more so than the achingly painful kneeboarding I tried later in the day and knew I'd never attempt again.

I was like a kid waiting for his birthday; I wanted that job so badly. Lisa phoned my office right after lunch the next day and suggested I come over and see how things worked in her shop. I walked over with my fingers crossed. I was hopeful that a job in JIG would help me figure this place out. I was especially eager to work with ICE—the interrogation control element—which oversaw the questioning of detainees. The army officer who headed the unit was respectfully known as the iceman.

Lisa told me right away that Major Richards had already talked to Captain Mansur, and the job was mine if I wanted it. Huge relief. As it turned out, now that they could tell me more, Lisa headed an office that coordinated and implemented certain intelligence collection needs on base. She supervised a group of between thirty and fifty civilian linguists—the number fluctuated—who cycled through her office. Lisa told me not to worry about the equipment in the room; her coworker Nadia was the technowhiz. When I asked about participating in interrogations, she told me to mention it to Major Richards, and I would get on the list. My new hours would be 1100 to 2000 weekdays and 0800 to 1300 Saturdays.

I would start in a couple of weeks, spending a few days with Lisa teaching me the ropes. I could certainly hang on at JDOG that much longer. It wasn't easy, however. In addition to all the bad team karma around me, the treatment of the detainees by the MPs had been degenerating. The IRF process had evolved over time with the help of the Connecticut 902nd. It was widely known that IRFs now were being used punitively, not just as a way to get detainees to comply with commands, which was their original purpose. Now if an MP walked down the cell-block and someone threw a cup of water or urine on him, he'd report it to the NCOIC, who would request an IRF team. And the IRF team would cast its net wide, going into the cells of three or four men nearest to where the incident had occurred.

And sometimes the IRFs got a little more violent. One day shortly before I switched teams, Mo took a call on Sierra block. I stopped by after I finished with another call to see if I could help. When I arrived, an IRF was about to take place in the rec yard. Mo was translating for the guard leadership while the IRF team waited to be called in to remove the detainee, who wanted a few more moments of freedom. I decided to watch from the rear cellblock steps, about twenty yards away from the entrance to the rec yard.

I asked the guard standing near me what had brought the IRF team out. "Usual situation. This detainee is claiming he hasn't been given sufficient time in the rec yard, so he is refusing to come out," he said. "He said he was ready for a fight." A little surprising, given that the detainee appeared to weigh less than 110 pounds and didn't have a muscular build.

When the IRF team moved to enter the yard, the detainees

on the cellblock started yelling in support of their man, "Allah al-Akbar" over and over. It was a mad scene. The next cellblock over joined in the shouting, creating even more chaos. I watched as the team knocked the detainee to the ground and swarmed him to put on the shackles. The detainees shouted obscenities at the guards, calling them American dogs and bastards. This guy was as thin as a rail but had decided to throw himself into resisting and screaming at the top of his lungs. Hatred bred disproportionate strength, and his shrieks only fueled the chaos inside the cellblock. As the guards struggled to make the detainee's arms conform to the shackles, I heard the unmistakable crack of a bone shattering.

Unfortunately, the detainees of cellblock Sierra heard the crack as well and believed that the guards had intentionally broken their brother's arm. His scream was ear piercing. The shouting intensified. Chants of Allah al-Akbar reverberated throughout the cell block. One detainee yelled, "They are snapping his arms like twigs!" Some of the men started shaking their doors and pounding their bare feet on the metal floor. Finally, the detainee was restrained, and the medics took him away on a stretcher for further examination. Mo went with them, and I was stuck trying to explain to the rioting detainees of Echo that the guards hadn't meant to break his arm.

"Listen," I said to one guy who seemed to be the cell leader, "as the respected leader, it is your responsibility to tell these men the truth, that the guards did not break his arm intentionally." At least I hoped this was the truth.

"You are a liar," he replied, looking at me with cold eyes.

"No, I'm not lying; they didn't break his arm on purpose. It was an accident—they were trying to get the handcuffs on him."

"Get away from me, soldier. Your lies sound just like the others."

It was a hopeless cause. The cellblock was still in full riot as I left.

One of the guards later told me that the detainee broke his own arm as he was resisting. But from that day forward the detainees believed that if the IRF team was headed their way, they would come out of it badly bashed up. When I asked Mo, who'd been at the camp a good deal longer than me, if he thought the guards would get in trouble once the leadership saw the videotape of the IRFing, he shrugged his shoulders. "The tape will disappear," he said. "That's what usually happens when things turn out like this." I never found out if that tape vanished.

Things were turning more and more to the liking of Ed Pagnotti, the tough-talking New York City cop and self-described Tony Soprano of the 902nd who believed in payback, ordered up good old-fashioned beatings, and did what he could to hide the evidence. I couldn't get away from JDOG quickly enough.

Before I left the blocks, I had another conversation with Mustapha. This orange-suited Syrian, sitting in a tiny jail cell, and I, an American soldier in combat boots, camouflage, and sunglasses, had talked a great deal by now about our respective faiths. Over time, I came to understand Mustapha's journey to radical Islam, from the streets of Damascus to the hills of Afghanistan and finally to an interrogation booth in a godforsaken carved-out corner of Cuba.

He'd been living a life of gambling and pursuing women in Syria. His family, he said, never prayed, fasted, or attended mosque. One day, a missionary knocked on his door. He asked Mustapha why he and his family didn't go to mosque, and explained that Islam teaches that God is to be feared and that one day he would face judgment. According to Mustapha, he was literally scared into believing; he didn't want to face God at the end of a life not lived according to the tenets of Islam. He became a follower of these missionaries and before long, according to him, he headed to Afghanistan to help them. Mustapha's newfound belief developed into a fanatical devotion. He fervently believed that true Muslims must practice violent jihad against the infidels, who included any non-Muslims. At the top of the list were Jews and Americans.

I asked him how his life was different now that he was committed to the cause. His response was very similar to words I had heard from many Christians, but with a twist. "Basam," he said, "before I got on the straight path, my life had no meaning. I was just wandering, with no purpose. And worse yet, I would have ended up facing the wrath of God. Now my life has meaning. I am devoted to something much greater than myself, the one true God. Because of that commitment, my life and my jihad will have an impact here on earth, in sha Allah, and I will go to paradise, in sha Allah." "In sha Allah," or God willing, is sprinkled through an extremely high percentage of conversations in Arabic.

I left the blocks convinced that conversations like those I had had with Mustapha had prepared me well for moving over to JIG. We had to understand the motivations of terrorists in order to find ways to make them willing to talk to us and to be able to sit with them face to face as human beings. I supposed the raw treatment the detainees were increasingly subjected to on the blocks might serve a short-term purpose, but I had a hard time seeing how it was serving our goals in the war on terror. And it had strengthened the resolve of many of them as much as it had broken the spirit of others. The fact that we had been imprisoning an unknown number of men for more than a year who had no significant connections to terrorism was to my mind a very bad fact. We had to hold to our own higher standards or we'd undermine everything we stood for. Fighting the terrorists was going to require a longer range, smarter strategy than we seemed to be deploying. They weren't going to go away anytime soon.

JIG

JOINT INTERROGATIONS GROUP

CHAPTER SEVEN

My old teammates jokingly called me *khaen*, "traitor," when I started my new job. Joining the JIG team was like sinking into a warm bath, a far cry from the interpersonal water torture of JDOG. The JIG linguists actually seemed to get along. I met most of them at a Saturday meeting and they all welcomed me warmly, as Lisa had predicted they would.

My main task was to run an audio communications unit* that was located in one of the same drab, utterly forgettable trailer-type shells that housed the JDOG linguists when they weren't on calls. I hadn't known this operation existed until Lisa briefed me. The linguists rotated through the office in shifts, about five or six at a time, when they weren't translating interrogations, and I supervised them and edited their work. Pentagon restrictions prevent me from describing exactly what we did, but most of the linguists found it tedious.

---

*This description of my duties is stated in my unclassified evaluation.

For me, it was anything but, at least at first. As the head of the office, I worked with not only military interrogators but also representatives of the FBI, DIA (Defense Intelligence Agency, the Pentagon's intel outfit), and our nation's largest overseas intelligence gathering agency, which I'm permitted to identify only as the other government agency (OGA). We coordinated to focus my office's efforts, and I shared the results with them.

This was much closer to what I had envisioned when I signed up for Gitmo duty. And now maybe I'd begin to get some answers to the questions that had been eating at me for some time: how much good intel were we getting from the captives, and how many of them really belonged there. I had full access to the computerized files of almost all of them, and I would be taking part in interrogations. Lisa had also told me that from time to time VIP visitors would shuttle through my office to see what we were all about. Donald Rumsfeld, the secretary of defense, and then army chief of staff General Eric Shinseki were two of the notables who had visited the base so far. Changing teams had been the best move of my military career.

I was supervising more than forty linguists, about double the number we'd had on the JDOG unit. We were all under Major Richards's command. Only about half a dozen or so were military. All the rest were American civilians, most of Middle Eastern birth or descent who spoke Arabic, Pashto, Urdu, or Farsi. Some were devout Muslims. We also had people who were fluent in more mainstream languages, like French or Russian, as well as some incredibly obscure ones, like Uighur, which is spoken by a Muslim ethnic group of the same name that had long been agitating for independence from China. They had been recruited to come to Gitmo by The Titan Corporation, a Pentagon contractor, and its subcontractors. Ranging in age from their early twenties to at least two who were in their sixties, they, like me, had liked the idea of helping in the fight against Usama and his allies. Frankly, the commitment of so many civilians to helping with the mission was impressive, and moving. They had been willing to walk away from their normal lives for months, leaving jobs and families and comfortable homes for the hellish heat and rough military lifestyle of Gitmo. They shared small bedrooms in crowded group houses and worked six days a week, often assisting interrogations in the middle of the night. At least they were paid pretty well, at a rate that would have worked out to about seventy thousand dollars a year.

In most cases, they or their parents had left the Middle East and found rewarding opportunities and a degree of personal freedom in the United States that they couldn't have imagined in their home countries. Many of them told me that when they signed on for Gitmo, it was because they wanted to give something back.

A couple of weeks after I'd joined JIG, General Miller, the camp commander, came by the team's regular Saturday meeting for a basic buck-'em-up appearance, to tell us we were doing a great job. He also helped Major Richards present awards to three of the civilian linguists who were heading back to the States after a year in Cuba. They had arrived in the early days, very soon after the first detainees were tossed into the cages of Camp X-ray.

General Miller wasn't generally considered a charmer. A

square-jawed Texan, he was said to be pugnacious and arrogant, and a screamer when he was angry. Some on the intel side questioned whether an infantry officer and artillery specialist was the right choice to head up a mission with a large intelligence-gathering component—prior to his arrival, the jobs of running camp operations and extracting intelligence had been under two different commanders. Still, he clearly had the leadership skills to know when to heap praise on civilians who had volunteered to parachute into a tough military scenario.

"These individuals did an outstanding job assisting the standing up of the camp," General Miller said, "and they were a critical part of the very beginning of the intelligence-gathering process that has helped us thwart future attacks and find suspected terrorists throughout the world."

One of the three departing linguists stood up when General Miller finished. He was a tall, thin, gray-haired Pashto speaker, probably in his late sixties. He had been born and raised in Afghanistan and still had family there. "Sir, you are thanking me for coming here, but in truth I don't know how to thank *you*," he said in thickly accented English. "What these people, these Taliban, have done to my country is horrible. They have tried to ruin a great and wonderful nation. But now my adopted home, America, has gone there to defeat these bastards." Tears were running down his face. "I could never thank you enough for getting rid of these people and letting me contribute to the war effort in some small way. Thank you." That might have been the first wholly positive thing I'd heard anyone say about the camp since I'd come. I was taken aback by his sincerity and the depth of his emotion, and by the time he had finished, my eyes were wet too.

Like the Muslim linguists on the JDOG team, these civilians had all been given interim security clearances, and with almost no training they'd been sent into sometimes intense interrogations with men accused of cold-blooded brutality who would almost certainly consider them traitors to their heritage.

On first impression, they seemed undisturbed, although I knew that as contractors, they felt less at liberty to discuss their personal views than some of my former colleagues. Their friendliness led them to ask a number of personal questions of *me*, though. They wanted to know about my family and, after they thought I'd had a chance to settle into the JIG office—they gave me a few hours—a few of the motherly Arab women among them started telling me that at age twenty-seven, I needed to hurry up and marry the pretty girl whose picture was taped to my computer.

A couple of interrogators also had offices in our trailer, but most of them were elsewhere. One of the linguists, Tim, a Russian speaker, coordinated the needs of the interrogators, who were divided up into five groups: Saudi Arabia; Pakistan and Afghanistan; Gulf states; Asia, Europe, and the Americas; and special projects. Tim drew up schedules for the linguists accordingly and posted assignments for the next day every evening at 1600.

My cosupervisor, Nadia, was the techy in charge of keeping our equipment (which I'm not permitted to describe) from going on the fritz. She was a fellow Fort Meade soldier, though we hadn't crossed paths there, and an Arabic linguist, but so far she had only used her college French in interrogations. She was quiet and mostly kept to herself, though despite her reticence, it was quickly apparent that she took a very dim view of the leadership at Camp Delta. She made repeated references to how "fucked up" the camp was. So the JIG group wasn't entirely a cloister of contentedness.

I wanted to find out who some of those guys I'd spent so much time around on the blocks really were, and what they had allegedly done. I knew, too, that there was at least one detainee I hadn't seen. Lisa had told me that the man referred to as the twentieth hijacker had been brought to the camp and was undergoing intensive interrogations. Mohamed al Qahtani, a Saudi, had tried to enter the United States via Orlando about a month before 9/11 but had been turned away by an immigration inspector because something about his story seemed off.* Every indication was that he was supposed to have been part of the operation, probably on the flight that crashed outside of Pittsburgh. The ringleader of the hijackers, Mohammed Atta, had been at the Orlando airport the day Qahtani landed; he was caught making a phone call by a surveillance camera. Qahtani was later captured in Afghanistan and was sent to Gitmo in late 2002. The twentieth hijacker was isolated at the old Camp X-ray, according to Lisa, and interrogators sometimes went at him for twenty hours straight, trying to get him to cough up details about how the 9/11 attacks were planned and carried out.

---

*Coauthor has established through sources other than me, including the *The 9/11 Commission Report*, that al Qahtani was the identity of the so-called twentieth hijacker.

In my first couple of weeks, I learned from looking at detainees' files and talking to interrogators that, besides the twentieth hijacker, we did indeed have some pretty bad actors at the camp, people who likely would have gone to some lengths to contribute to additional attacks, and we had ample reasons to think they were terrorists or terrorist facilitators. I'm restricted from providing details about what I saw, or what the interrogators had gotten out of them, but there was a concerted effort to try to get these relatively high-value detainees to tell us about other key players within Al Qaeda, about their financing, the locations of safe houses around the world, and especially other planned attacks.

Others were hardly terrorist operatives, but had useful info they were sharing. Among them were six Iraqi Shiite Muslims. I had heard about them on the blocks. They were reviled by the rest of the detainee population, primarily because of religious differences—most of the captives were Sunni, and the bad blood between Sunnis and Shiites goes back through the ages. But many also suspected them, I now learned with good reason, of cooperating with their interrogators and turning in those whom they believed, often from conversations they heard on the cellblocks, had trained with Al Qaeda. Sultan and the other five Shiites could be laughably overt about trying to get the goods on other inmates, attempting to engage them in conversations about where they were from and what they did. Word was that Ali, another of them, sang like a bird, telling his interrogators anything and everything. He may have been making up half of it, though. Ali was obviously all about portraying himself in a favorable light.

Now I learned more of their stories, which were all similar.

Sultan, for instance, had fled Iraq because he didn't want to do his compulsory service in Saddam's army (Saddam Hussein was a Sunni, and Shiites, though they were in the majority, were treated like second-class citizens). Sultan made it to Iran, but was caught by authorities there and booted out. Rather than return to Iraq, he chose to try his luck to the east—Afghanistan. Soon, though, the Taliban, who were Sunnis, caught him and took him in for questioning and torture, believing he was an Iranian spy. He had the burn marks to prove it.

Eventually the Taliban believed Sultan, and he even convinced them that his education and knowledge of agriculture could be helpful to them. He was put in charge of some poppy fields. Within a few years he had two wives, two children, and was living happily ever after. Then one day, according to him, a Taliban official came by and told everyone to take up arms; the infidels were coming. Sultan, having no TV or radio, didn't know about September 11, he said, and had no idea what the official was talking about. Suddenly his fields were being bombed. He saw troops moving in, and he surrendered to the Northern Alliance as soon as they arrived.

Ali, like Sultan, had fled Iraq to avoid military service, and had headed east after being bounced out of Iran. In Afghanistan he tried to make his way as a skilled jack-of-all-trades, and eventually he got a job in an Al Qaeda training facility fixing broken toilets and doing other janitorial tasks. He married, had a family, and lived a passable life side by side in the camp with Al Qaeda trainees. When the Northern Alliance came, he was rounded up with all the others and turned over to the Americans. He wasn't a terrorist, but he did have valuable information to impart.

The interrogators were perfectly open about rewarding this group: they sometimes brought Sultan and the others food from McDonald's, which they'd eat in front of the other detainees, and of course the smell of those burgers and fries probably traveled all the way down the cellblock. Ali was one of the few inmates who was given magazines. One day he showed one, an issue of *Maxim*, to Mark, who was shocked that any detainee was allowed to read that kind of magazine. More shocking was that when Ali showed Mark the inside, it turned out to be *Playboy*, with a *Maxim* cover. "I'll do anything they ask as long as they keep giving me this porn," Ali had said.

It got so bad that the Sunni detainees issued a fatwa against the Shiites.

From what I was seeing in the files, though, detainees with valuable information weren't the norm. I was amazed that some of the files I was looking at were so thin—sometimes just a mug shot, an ID number from Bagram, and a summary of the detainee's initial interrogation, which might say that he had maintained he was a farmer, that he denied any connection to terrorism, and claimed to have been picked up by the Northern Alliance or the Pakistanis. Of course, if the American military had picked him up, we would have known that, so this last claim at least was verifiable.

Unfortunately, the others were tougher. Many of the thinner files belonged to detainees who were cooperative in interrogations but seemed honestly not to know much, and a lot of them insisted that they had never heard of Al Qaeda. As we had all noticed when I was part of JDOG, there were also quite a few detainees who were no longer being grilled.

Another thing that quickly became obvious from my new vantage point was that there were some hammer-and-tongs turf wars going on in the camp among the different agencies questioning the detainees. The FBI, DIA, and OGA fought with one another and with the military interrogators over who would get access to a captive. They didn't trust each other, and the FBI and OGA had an especially contentious relationship. The military tended to be the low man on the totem pole—if one of the other agencies wanted dibs, it could put a detainee on hold so he couldn't be questioned by the military. That really bugged the MI soldiers, since Camp Delta was an army-run installation.

The interrogators were under a lot of pressure to extract from the captives the golden nuggets that would prevent future terrorist attacks. But it took their very best efforts to get some of the detainees to do anything other than stare at the walls or complain about how the guards treated them, or simply say they didn't know anything. And it was crystal clear to me and anyone else paying attention that very little of the interagency intelligence sharing that was supposed to be taking place in the aftermath of 9/11 had made its way to Cuba; I suspected that that was more talk than action even on the mainland. It was the same old story: everybody was worried about looking good.

Around the time I started at JIG, two FBI special agents came to the island to question a high-priority detainee. It turned out that he was the detainee I had heard earlier was such a charismatic teacher that he was given immediate respect on whichever cellblock he was moved to. Muhammad Salahi was a North African who had spent time in Canada and Germany.* I wasn't the linguist for the agents' sessions with him, but I was helping them with their project.

The military interrogators were openly pissed about not being able to interview this detainee. After the agents had been questioning him for several weeks, I heard one of the MI interrogators venting to his warrant officer about the FBI's strategy. Ben was a thirtyish army staff sergeant and interrogator from New York, and he tended to be unpleasant. He seemed like the type who had always been picked on in school and joined the army to turn the tables.

"Those goddamn agents sit in chairs across the table and talk to the guy all night like they were chatting with their best friend," said Ben. He clearly had very different tactics in mind. "The one dude is actually growing a beard. I think he's converting, for God's sake." Ben was right about the beard. One of the agents had decided to mimic the North African and many other Muslims in this respect, as a sort of show of respect for their faith.

"When are we going to get our hands on that bastard, sir?" Ben finished.

"I can't imagine they'll stick with it much longer," the warrant officer said. "They can't keep fooling themselves."

---

*Coauthor has learned details about Salahi, including his detention at Guantánamo, through sources other than me.

But the FBI agents burrowed into their case like moles. They asked everyone in sight, including me, questions about Islam, to try to better understand their subject's belief system and what he might consider offensive. They even learned a little Arabic. And that beard grew quite full. They wound up staying three months, during which the detainee, who had been as cynical as they come in the beginning, seemed to become more receptive. He was a smart guy and knew they were trying to exploit him, but he also sensed that they really wanted to understand his language, culture, and religion. I wasn't sure exactly how much they were getting out of our important captive—I had access to his file, but it hadn't been updated with their reports. Still, judging from my conversations with these persistent agents, it was obvious they were making progress.

As much as the army interrogators hated it, it made sense for them to go last. They were generally the least experienced of the lot, having received their training in a sixteen-week course, or sometimes less, at Fort Huachuca. Until 9/11, graduates of the program had usually been sprinkled among various army divisions around the world to be on hand in case of war. The lower-ranking ones often had to do mundane tasks like vehicle maintenance, cut the grass, fill sandbags, and so on—the sort of thing I had been muttering about the day the planes hit—while occasionally participating in mock interrogations. Once they moved up the ladder, their duties would improve, but in any case, before the 2001 attacks, very, very few army interrogators had ever questioned a suspected terrorist or POW.

General Miller liked to refer to Gitmo as the "testing lab in the global war on terrorism," and told journalists that he preferred interrogators with between two and six years in the service. "Intelligence is a young person's game," he said, touting the flexibility of youth. To my mind, the problem with his view was that it devalued experience. Miller was squandering a terrific opportunity, I thought.

Camp Delta would have been great training for the military interrogators if they'd been assigned to work more closely with those from the FBI and OGA, some of whom had been questioning for years individuals connected to terrorist enterprises in cases like the first World Trade Center bombing in 1993, the Khobar Towers bombing in Saudi Arabia in 1996, the 1998 bombings of the American embassies in Kenya and Tanzania, and the 2000 attack on the USS *Cole* in Yemen. But instead of having its interrogators sit in and learn from them, the military just resented the presence of the other organizations. Knowing the army the way I'd come to understand it, I was sure it was an issue of pride.

It was also pride, of course, as well as outright self-preservation, that made it so important to put the best possible face on the camp when VIPs came to visit. A façade would go up, like a set in an old movie. We'd put on quite a show—the camp's leadership had these events down to a science.

When a group of intel professionals from the government's senior executive service—some of the most proficient intelligence experts we have—came for a visit, we got the itinerary days beforehand, learned exactly what they wanted to see, and my commanders staged the production carefully. These visitors always wanted to sit in the observation room outside an interrogation booth, watching through the one-way glass. A flurry of e-mails went back and forth among JIG staff about which detainee to schedule for these observations and what to ask him. The key was to pick someone who had already been cooperative, and the interrogator would simply go back over material covered with him previously. A foolproof recipe for faux interrogations and the VIPs were none the wiser.

All of us who briefed the visiting celebrities were encouraged to highlight the positive and downplay any difficulties. In my office, I was pressed to hype what we produced so General Miller could justify the $3 million worth of equipment we were using.* Whenever General Miller entered my cramped working quarters with some VIPs, he'd say, "This office uses state-of-the-art technology and its phenomenal work provides a direct benefit to the global war on terrorism." Every single time General Miller referred to the war, it was the *global* war on terrorism. I knew nobody else who so robotically attached the four words of the term together each time he mentioned it.

General Miller continued to assert that we were holding "the worst of the worst" and getting top-quality intelligence out of our operation, but that wasn't the reality I was seeing. I started to feel as though I were living in a Potemkin village, like the elaborate fake towns the eighteenth-century Russian field marshal rushed to build when Catherine the Great toured her empire. General Miller's overstatements, I thought, made the real intel professionals lose respect for him.

Every other weekend, my new colleagues threw a party ei-

---

*The dollar value of the equipment is stated in my unclassified evaluation.

ther in the carport of one of the linguist's houses or down on the beach, with wonderful food, music, and dancing. They had the kind of camaraderie you hoped for when you were so far from home with others in the same shipwrecked environment, the kind my old teammates had never managed to find.

One Saturday soon after I started, I was invited to a party at the home of a few of the civilians. Some of the older gentlemen were taking care of the grill while the women were busy setting up the other food and making sure that everyone was stuffing themselves silly.

I grabbed a drink and sat in a lawn chair in the driveway with Mark, whom I'd brought to the gathering, and Ahmed Mehalba, a thirtyish linguist who had previously been in the army and on track to become an interrogator when he had to leave the service for medical reasons. Born in Egypt, he had moved to the United States when he was young but grew up speaking Arabic at home; his language skills were superior. He was extremely congenial, always had a smile on his face, and seemed to be one of the best workers in our lineup. Two of the women civilian linguists I supervised were also there. Ameena was a very kind, Syrian-born woman in her early forties who made fantastic baklava. She said it made her smile to hear me speak Arabic (I was afraid that was because she found it comical). Leila was a young, Egyptian-born woman with an NYU degree in communications who had worked as a traffic reporter for a New York City radio station before she became a linguist. Ben, the army interrogator, joined us. Our conversation reinforced my earlier impression that he had a chip on his shoulder.

Our talk—the usual camp gossip—turned to a discussion

about interrogations and techniques. At one point, Ameena asked Ben, "What kind of rules do you guys have to follow?"

"They're flexible," Ben said. "We sort of operate on a case-by-case basis."

Mehalba asked Ben, "I've worked in a few interrogations where it seems as if we don't know anything about the detainee. Isn't there some sort of screening process before a detainee is sent here? How do we know all of these guys are guilty?"

"Look, you're right," Ben said. "We have no idea how some of these motherfuckers got here. But the truth is, most of them in one way or another were supporters of either the Taliban or Al Qaeda. If a few of 'em got here by mistake, I'm sorry, but this is war and I'm not going to lose sleep over it. They'll get home eventually."

I jumped in, cleverly inviting Ben to take my head off. "Doesn't that seem sort of contradictory to the values we signed up to defend?"

"What's the matter with you, Saar?" he said. "Yeah, in a perfect world we, as an army, would always perfectly reflect and defend the values of this country. But hey, join us in reality. If you're going to worry about bullshit like whether a few of the detainees need to be here or exactly how we talk to them, you're going to have a rough time." Ben didn't want any more of this. He headed for the cooler to grab another beer, then joined another conversation.

"I'm really sorry that we upset him," said Ameena.

"You know," I said, "I think these guys feel tons of pressure to get information from the detainees, and sometimes they just strike out. I'm sure it's easy to fly off the handle when you're in that position." We sat around for a while longer, eating and drinking. I felt almost relieved. There were others among my new colleagues who shared my concerns. Nobody, though, at least not that I'd heard about, had decided to voice those doubts to anyone above the rank of major.

CHAPTER EIGHT

One morning in February, the entire JIG team was summoned to a meeting across base at what everyone referred to as the yellow office building. The building primarily held administrative offices, but rumors were circulating that part of it would soon be converted to a courtroom. It had been more than a year since President Bush had signed off on the special military commission system for accused terrorists, but to date not a single one of the detainees had been charged and we all wondered when things would get moving. Early on, the rules for the commissions (sometimes called tribunals) had come under fire from civil libertarians and many lawyers, mainly because they stacked the deck so heavily in the government's favor. Prosecutors would be permitted to introduce evidence under looser standards than civilian courts allowed, for example, and it would take the votes of only two thirds of the jurors, rather than all of them, to convict a defendant. And there would be no way to appeal a judgment to an independent body outside the military's chain of command, a key restriction that drew more objections than any other.

I was hoping this meeting would bring us up to speed on how the detainees would be brought to justice. It was a major source of irritation, not only for the captives but for the camp personnel, that we lacked an organized procedure for determining which of them should stay and which should go. It was past time to separate the wheat from the chaff. This wasn't just a moral issue, it was a practical one. It would be easier for the intel personnel to focus on the real terrorists once the others had been sent home.

Nadia and I filed into the darkened auditorium and took seats among our intel colleagues: about a hundred linguists, interpreters, intelligence analysts, and their leadership. We didn't fill even half of the cushioned black chairs in the room. Colonel Russell Simms, the top intelligence officer on the base, stood up, and the first frame of the obligatory Power-Point presentation lit up the screen behind him. It's a fundamental of army life that no briefing is complete without a PowerPoint show. "I know some of you have wondered how Camp Delta fits into our nation's legal establishment," he began. "Today we have a JAG attorney here to lay that out for you." Colonel Simms was in his midfifties with a full head of cropped white hair. He wore glasses and looked like a college professor. "This same presentation was recently given to some very high-ranking officials in Washington, including the head of the DIA," the colonel said. "I hope Captain Henderson will be able to answer some of your questions and fill in some blanks for you."

Captain Henderson looked like every other JAG (short for Judge Advocate General) lawyer I'd seen in my army career. He was probably in his early thirties, with short dark hair and brown eyes, fairly nondescript. Yet there's something about most military lawyers that you can't put your finger on—if you saw him around the base, you would know he was JAG because he didn't quite fit in. The captain spent the next half hour talking not about military tribunals, but the relevance of the Geneva Conventions at Camp Delta—or irrelevance, in this case. More precisely, he told us that the Third and Fourth Geneva Conventions of 1949, which deal with treatment of prisoners of war and civilians, didn't apply to the more than six hundred suspected Al Qaeda and Taliban figures we had locked up here in the Caribbean. "These detainees can't be considered prisoners of war in the conventional sense," he told us. We knew that they were being called "unlawful combatants" and that President Bush had signed an order the previous February to that effect. Geneva didn't apply, he wrote, because "the war against terrorism ushers in a new paradigm." But his order had also said that the military "shall continue to treat detainees humanely and, to the extent appropriate and consistent with military necessity, in a manner consistent with the principles of Geneva." At that time, it hadn't seemed to me like much would change.

Now Captain Henderson and his PowerPoint sidekick gave us the reasons why, according to the Bush administration, these individuals hadn't earned their POW bona fides. For one, he said, they didn't have an identifiable command structure like the armed forces of other nations. Second, they didn't follow the rules of conventional warfare—they might target civilians as well as opposing fighters, for instance. And third, they didn't wear uniforms.

I dutifully followed each bullet on the screen, but it surprised me that we were being given rationales for the decision about Geneva. This meeting was an explainer, and the military doesn't do explainers. It quickly dawned on me, though, that the reason we were getting this dog-and-pony show was that this was so huge. This wasn't just dry information about paper classification of the guys in the blaze-orange outfits. This was an issue the military, and the higher-ups in the administration, clearly felt was dicey enough that they had to stoop to providing us with some reasons, such as they were. Maybe more was changing than I had thought.

Colonel Simms got back up when Captain Henderson was done to reinforce what the lawyer had said. "We still intend to treat the detainees humanely," he noted, "but our purpose is to get any actionable intelligence we can, and quickly." There was no Q and A.

In my time at Gitmo, I hadn't once heard the term *prisoner* used. The captives were *detainees*, a word that had seemed stiff and unnatural when I'd arrived. This was why. To call them prisoners would be too close to calling them POWs, which would be akin to saying they were protected by international law. It was a game of semantics. That was one question answered.

Otherwise, our session with Captain Henderson only raised

more questions for me, lots of them. I knew the drill that a good soldier just does what he's told and leaves the strategizing to the big guys. But this briefing was nothing but spin. I hopped back in the van along with Nadia and a few of the other JIG military linguists. "Well, I've never had a briefing like that before," Nadia said, "and I've been in the army six years." Major Richards, who was driving, didn't seem to want to discuss it. "I wouldn't read too much into that, guys," she said. "It was what it was."

Cued to change the topic, everyone started talking about weekend plans. But I kept thinking about the meeting and growing more pissed. It's always set me off to be treated as if I'm on the low end of the IQ scale ever since my older sisters used to persecute me by saying, "You're retarded—it even says so on your birth certificate." In the intel world that usually didn't happen; you were expected to be on your toes and you were treated as though you were. Here, though, I felt as if we were being fed bullshit, that I was being asked to accept a dodge-and-weave treatment of the Geneva rules.

I had seen the files of many men who claimed to be, and apparently were, conscripts for the Taliban. They argued that they were forced to fight simply because they were of age. The United States had exposed to the world what a despicable group the Taliban was; we had spread the word that they were oppressing the Afghani people. We knew it was true that they would have killed those who refused to fight. But now we at Gitmo were being told that if only they had been able to throw together some ragged uniforms, they might be POWs instead of enemy combatants. And the command structure in

Afghanistan might have been fluid, but what wasn't in that hapless, stone-broke rock pile of a country? What about the guys who really were in the wrong place at the wrong time, rounded up by opportunists who collected handsome rewards for their prey from the United States? It didn't hold up.

At bottom, of course, this was all about how we did interrogations. Although Colonel Simms hadn't been explicit, it was clear that the rules for questioning detainees were going to be looser, if they weren't already. Was this all happening because after more than a year, the interrogators still weren't getting the kind of intel we'd hoped for? After my first few weeks at JIG, I still hadn't taken part in any interrogations, but I'd heard a fair amount from linguists and interrogators around the office. An army linguist who had participated in questioning the so-called twentieth hijacker told me that military dogs were used to intimidate him. Our psy-ops people—the Behavioral Science Consultation Team, called Biscuit—plastered the walls of his interrogation booth with pictures of those who were killed on 9/11; the interrogator asked him if this was what his religion was all about. He was subjected to strobe lights; a loud, insistent tape of cats meowing (from a cat food commercial) interspersed with babies crying; and deafening loud music—one song blasted at him constantly was Drowning Pool's thumping, nihilistic metal rant "Bodies" ("Let the bodies hit the floor . . ."). Those procedures had been approved for Mohamed al Qahtani by Donald Rumsfeld. Were we applying tactics like that more broadly?

One big problem was that whatever the new rules were, nobody had any experience with them. In the army you're trained for every event. No detail is too minor. Training, in fact, is all the army does when it isn't actually at war. I knew that the military's interrogators had been trained to question prisoners strictly within the confines of the Geneva Conventions. The Army Field Manual describes in detail the types of techniques that are in compliance with Geneva, which says that "no physical or mental torture, nor any other form of coercion, may be inflicted on prisoners of war to secure from them information of any kind whatever. Prisoners of war who refuse to answer may not be threatened, insulted, or exposed to unpleasant or disadvantageous treatment of any kind." And any interrogator will tell you that those rules are burned into their military heads, with a reinforcing adage: torture doesn't work, and in fact produces less reliable information because it has a tendency to induce victims to lie. Interrogators were taught that if they were skilled, they could get all the information they needed without going too far.

I resented the discomfort I was feeling. As we drove back to camp, I argued the other side with myself too. This is war against an unconventional adversary, you pussy, so maybe they're right; maybe we need new principles to beat the terrorists. We can't meet them on the battlefield, not in the usual sense, so maybe they've forced us to change the rules in other ways too. Earlier in my stint at Gitmo, that reasoning would have won the day. But by this time, I'd seen too much of the reality, or unreality, of the camp. I knew too much to kid myself, and I didn't take well to being asked to pretend that what I'd just been told made good military sense. I also had no confidence that the longer-term consequences of this policy had been thought through. If we were more casual about the Geneva Convention with our captives, how would our soldiers be treated when they were captured? What kind of brutality might we be visiting upon ourselves in the future fight?

This was, of course, great fodder for the critics of the administration's post-9/11 actions, both at home and globally, who argued that the United States was acting in ways that were at odds with the principles it claimed to stand for. I hadn't generally agreed with them in the past. They weren't on the scene and didn't know the real score. I had proudly slapped a Bush-Cheney sticker on my door at Fort Huachuca in 2000, and thought Bush had been an outstanding leader in the immediate aftermath of the attacks; many of the criticisms, I believed, were politically motivated.

But now I was starting to feel different. I took my duty to the army extremely seriously, and I was going to have to find a way to justify to myself the legality of our operation, to reconcile my beliefs as an American, my conscience, and my religious beliefs with my duty as a soldier. That cursory PowerPoint run-through had shaken me, and I wished I hadn't attended.

Late one afternoon soon after the Geneva meeting, Tim, our scheduler, called and asked if I wanted to work an interrogation with the OGA the next day. Absolutely, I told him. This would be my first chance to actually see what the sessions were like, and I was glad it would be with the more experienced OGA at the helm.

The OGA preferred to work with MI linguists whenever

possible because we held the top secret clearances granted only after extensive background investigations, whereas the civilian linguists held only interim secret clearances. In most cases, their background checks were still in the process of being completed. The OGA representative would pick me up at my house the next day, Tim said, and our session probably wouldn't last more than two hours. "Oh," said Tim before he hung up, "wear civilian clothes."

In the morning I waited outside the house in khaki pants and a navy-blue golf shirt. At exactly the scheduled time the interrogator pulled into my driveway in a gray sedan. My first surprise was that an attractive girl in her late twenties, with long brown hair, was behind the wheel. I felt like a knucklehead for expecting some dated stereotype, a standoffish guy with graying hair in his midforties.

Michelle, it turned out, was a graduate of the University of Pennsylvania with a degree in finance, and she grew up in the state too, so we quickly found common ground. She was extremely friendly and very bright. She told me the guy we'd be "interviewing" that day was a Moroccan who spoke some Spanish; since Michelle spoke Spanish fluently, she thought she might get the opportunity to use her language skills, but she needed me along in case he preferred to speak in Arabic. He'd been picked up in Afghanistan by the Northern Alliance, and foreign intelligence services reported that he had suspicious connections to a known European Al Qaeda operative. Michelle's task was to determine the validity of the reported link. In the first session, she said, she planned to simply try to get to know him and build rapport.

My next surprise was the setting for this encounter. The

OGA trailer was furnished with a sofa, a coffee table strewn with magazines, a refrigerator with an ample supply of bottled water and soda, and a large stash of cigarettes. The furniture was a couple of decades old, not in the greatest shape, but far more comfortable than the detainee would have seen in quite a while. When he was brought to the room, Michelle told the MPs to remove his chains and asked the detainee to have a seat on the couch. "Are you sure, ma'am?" one of the MPs said, apprehensive about leaving a suspected terrorist completely unbound. She assured him she knew what she was doing and told them they could wait outside.

The detainee sat down and Michelle introduced herself and me in Spanish. "I understand you speak some Spanish. Do you want me to talk to you in Spanish or would you rather we use Arabic?"

The detainee looked at me and said in Arabic that although he knew some Spanish, he'd rather converse in his mother tongue. I translated. "No problem," Michelle said.

As we settled into our seats Michelle said, "Abdulla, would you like a Coke?" He appeared surprised and said, "Thank you," accepting her offer.

"My colleague and I are both from the northeastern part of the United States," she continued. "We look forward to getting to know you a bit, and we plan to talk to you in an atmosphere of respect." This last part seemed to have a deeper meaning that I didn't understand at the time. Apparently, Michelle wanted to separate herself from the military and the techniques they may have used when they spoke with the detainees.

Michelle offered him a cigarette, and he took her up on that as well. She tried to convince him that we were trying to learn the truth and that we had no preconceived opinions about his guilt or innocence.

"I'm glad you mentioned that," he said, "because I have no idea why I'm here." The truth was that we weren't sure either, but then that's what we were there to find out.

"We just want to learn more about you and talk to you about some of the people you met when you were living in Spain," she said.

'You mean you don't want to know why I was in Afghanistan?" he said skeptically. "You're not going to spend hours telling me I'm a liar and a bad Muslim? This is what the army does," referring to the MI interrogators. "They keep telling me that they know I'm Al Qaeda and I'm lying about going to Afghanistan to work and see my brother."

"I'm not the army," Michelle said crisply. "Why don't you tell us about your family and your life growing up in Morocco?"

He was resistant at first, but Michelle told him a bit about her own family (which was probably great fiction) to break the ice. Eventually he started to open up. She asked him about schools he had attended, how he got along with his two brothers and sister, what his brothers did for a living, what his family's religious practices were.

The detainee claimed that his family had been very secular when he was a child. After high school, he had spent a few years in Spain and at one point was convicted of stealing. That sent him back to Morocco, where he found that his family was now attending mosque on a regular basis and his brother was considering going to Afghanistan. He, too, started to attend mosque every Friday out of fear of Judgment Day.

After about two hours of this kind of conversation, Michelle thanked him for his time and asked how he would feel about talking to us again the following week. He was confused because she seemed to be seeking his permission. "You are actually asking me if I want to talk to you again?" he asked.

"Yes," said Michelle, standing up to gather her things. "I want to know how you feel about seeing us again."

"That would be fine," said the Moroccan. "I would much rather talk to you than the army interrogators."

"Great," said Michelle. "We'll see you next week."

Leaving the interview, I reflected that I was a novice, but I was impressed with Michelle's approach. Maybe it was some of my old marketing and sales background coming into play, but I could see how skillfully, and how quickly, Michelle had built a bridge to the detainee. She seemed to break down the typical barriers he would have raised and was able to get him to talk. It was clear, at least in this case, that Michelle's approach was highly effective. The next day I got to see a different way of attacking the problem.

It had been a smooth shift and it was just about 2000 hours, time to knock off, when Tim called. "Hey," he said, "I need a linguist to work a DOD interrogation tonight around 2200. Do you want to help out?" This would be with an MI interrogator, which I thought would be interesting.

"Sure, no problem," I said.

"Just be sure to cover your name." For this interrogation I'd be wearing my uniform. "You'll be working with Ben."

While I threw some Hot Pockets in the microwave for a quick dinner back home, Mark described a near riot in the cellblocks earlier that day, instigated when one of the MPs had dropped a Koran and the detainees went nuts. "It was crazy!" Mark said. "They were throwing so much water at the guards that they decided to shut it off for the afternoon. Their chow holes were open, and they all bunched up their mattresses and pushed them through into the wet hallway." Mark was talking about the openings in the detainees' cell doors that were unlocked just before mealtimes to hand in the food, the same openings we'd used to give them their flu shots. "Meanwhile, I'm down there talking to the detainees, trying to explain that the guard didn't mean any disrespect. It was quite a day." I couldn't say I missed life on the cellblocks.

I gulped my food and jumped in the van again to head back to Delta. As I walked across the camp parking lot and up to the gate, I was more aware than usual of bleakness against beauty. It was a perfect night with clear skies, lots of stars visible, and an ocean breeze, probably 70 degrees. The insufferable daytime weather often gave way to fine evenings at Guantánamo. As always, blocking what would have been a gorgeous view of the ocean was a sea of concertina wire and the glaring spotlights mounted around the perimeter of the camp.

Before my session with Michelle, she had explained that she'd simply be trying to get to know our subject. When I found Ben, I asked him what the upcoming interrogation would be like. He acted as if I was out of line for posing the question and clearly had no intention of explaining anything to me. "Just translate," he said.

The man in shackles was already waiting for us in the interrogation booth, a bare room with a couple of folding chairs and a D ring in the linoleum floor. One wall had a window of one-way glass, opaque to us; on the other side was a small observation room, almost certainly unoccupied, as was usually the case. The air-conditioning was turned up too high. The captive's ankle chains had been shortened and attached to the ring so there was no play in his feet, and a short chain connected his handcuffs to the ring as well. The arrangement forced him to hunch over, partially squatting. He appeared to have been there a while.

We took our seats in the folding chairs and Ben stared at the detainee for a good two minutes without saying a word. It wasn't clear to me what his intent was. Ben was anything but an imposing figure. He was about five foot eight, slightly pudgy, with a receding hair line. But I figured he must have a plan.

"Are you going to cooperate tonight?" Ben finally asked calmly. The detainee stared at the wall.

"Why were you in Afghanistan?"

Again nothing.

"What the fuck are you looking at, asshole? Answer the goddamn question! Why were you in Kandahar, you terrorist fuck?"

The detainee looked at me and said, "I've told him before; I was in Afghanistan to teach the Koran to the Afghan people."

"Stop lying to me," Ben said.

The conversation continued this way for a good half hour. Ben asked the detainee the same question again and again, and the detainee gave the same answer.

"Listen," Ben said, "I can stay here all night. All you have to do is answer my question; tell the truth and we can sit here and talk like men."

Nothing.

"Tell me why you were in Afghanistan."

Nothing.

"What is your fucking problem?" Ben shouted as he stood up. "Do you want to stay here the rest of your life?"

Nothing.

Ben sat back down and tried to look the detainee in the eye, but he avoided Ben. "Listen to me, you little bitch, I'm going to make you hate life! Do you understand? Start talking! Why were you in Afghanistan?"

No response.

Ben called the detainee a liar and every obscenity in the book. A few times when Ben would say something, he and I would make eye contact and he'd see me looking perplexed. After a half hour of the same shit Ben got up, kicked his chair, and stormed out of the room. I assumed this was my cue to follow him, but I half wondered if maybe Ben's show of anger was a ploy and now I was supposed to stay and start being really nice to the guy. But he'd given me no hint that was the plan, so I went out into the hall. As the door shut behind me I looked at Ben. He sensed my bewilderment. "Just translate the fucking interrogation," he said, looking me in the eye. "I don't need shit from you too."

Ben decided to take a break for about an hour while the detainee remained hunched in his exceedingly uncomfortable position in the booth. When we went back in around 2330 we replayed the previous questioning for another half hour.

Shortly after midnight Ben ended the interrogation. "We have all the time in the world," he told the detainee. "We can do this every night if you want to."

We left the booth and Ben walked across the hall to his office without saying a word. I yelled in to him, "Are we done?"

"Yep," he said nonchalantly.

When I left the building, I noticed a shackled detainee walking over near the clinic, being led by an MP. I had seen this on a couple of other occasions when I'd been at the camp late at night. These walkabouts in the small hours were used to keep detainees awake, sometimes in preparation for an interrogation that would take place even later.

In the last twenty-four hours I had been clued in to at least one reason why the OGA and military interrogators barely spoke to each other. Driving home for the second time that night, I wondered whether the base hospital would treat this particular kind of whiplash.

CHAPTER NINE

The ironies of life at Delta were many. One of them was the JIG team beach party, which over time had turned into something of a Middle Eastern version of a Hawaiian luau: lots of food and dancing, but no bikinis. We all needed ways to cope with the stresses and assorted absurdities of the camp, and this was one of my favorites. These parties became legendary on the island because of the phenomenal cooking and the way the dancing and music transported you to a garden of Middle Eastern delight, an oasis in the banana rat–infested, tension-riddled desert of Guantánamo.

The parties were down at a pavilion on Windmill Beach, usually on Saturday afternoons and stretching well into the night. I have no idea how people found the ingredients at the base NEX to make such delicious shawarma, stuffed grape leaves, tabbouleh, the best hummus you could ever eat, and mouth-watering baklava.

As the music played and the wine flowed, many of the women on my linguist team would take to the pavilion patio and begin to dance in an almost trancelike style I had never seen before—their arms waving and their hips swaying smoothly and sensually. Occasionally some men would join in, but they usually kept a respectful distance.

Everyone left the parties overstuffed, unable to resist the nurturing Arab women incessantly saying "Eat, eat . . ." I felt swept up in the warm hospitality of the Middle East, just as I had when my instructors at DLI had opened their homes to their students and immersed us in the richness of their cultures. A good time had by all, and much needed.

Translating for interrogations defied any expectations I might have had, and was so different from my old work on JDOG that I might as well have come from a job preparing tax returns. On the cellblocks, often as not I just talked to a detainee myself and didn't have to directly translate anything. If I was the intermediary between a detainee and a medic, MP, or psych tech, I had to stay with the meaning of what was said but could put it in my own words. In interrogations, though, I had to channel the interrogator—precise words, tone of voice, mood, even physical motions—and sometimes that took quite a bit of doing. Sometimes that made me want to punch a wall.

One afternoon before Lisa left the island, I asked her if the linguists went through any sort of training for interrogations. "No," she said, "we just give them a short briefing when they arrive. There are three things they need to remember. First, they are never to question the interrogator. Two, they should always stay 'in character.' In other words, if the interrogator is leaning back in his chair and speaking softly, then the linguist should do the same. If the interrogator stands up and screams, the linguist should do the same. And three, they should do their best to translate word for word and not try to add what they think the interrogator is trying to say."

She told me that with those of us in MI, the interrogators might choose to consult a little more about strategy or give us the fill on what they were going after. But some would not. The drill was to go in and turn yourself into whatever interrogator you happened to be teamed with that night; come out, turn back into yourself, and don't talk to anyone about what had transpired inside. After working my first several sessions, I came to think of us linguists as a little like kids in a completely dysfunctional family. At home, behind closed doors, you just do your best to survive and speak only when spoken to; on the outside, you don't dare tell anyone how fucked up it is back home.

Facing an alleged terrorist eye to eye was no longer a big deal. I'd been talking to them for months back on the blocks. The challenging part was stepping into someone else's shoes, not only speaking his or her words, but using the same mannerisms and manipulations in the same ways: swearing with the right degree of disgust or rage, cajoling with the right degree of guile. It was especially difficult when I couldn't fathom how the interrogator thought he or she was going to be getting anywhere.

Working with Michelle was not a problem. She was highly trained and seemed to have a natural gift for establishing connections. She was a people person, like me. We worked with the detainee from Morocco several more times. Michelle was in a tough spot because her headquarters was under pressure to nail down his alleged link to the European Al Qaeda member, and yet she had no hard information to question him about and no evidence whatsoever to prod him with. He claimed and claimed again that he'd been rounded up by the Northern Alliance simply because he was an Arab. What could she say to refute him? As with so many of the captives we'd apprehended through the NA, we knew nothing at all about what his involvement with Al Qaeda or the Taliban was supposed to have been.

We questioned another detainee who was of great interest to a foreign government I'm not at liberty to identify, but as with the Moroccan, we couldn't verify either that government's assertions about his activities or his denials. An interesting twist to this case was that the captive worked for Aljazeera, the Qatar-based Arabic news network. When Michelle and I arrived for our first encounter with him, she grabbed two Cokes and told me to take what I wanted from the well-stocked fridge. "This guy may not be too happy with us," she warned me.

We walked into the room where the detainee apparently had just arrived. Michelle told the MP to remove the man's shackles and leave the trailer. She slid a Coke across the table to him. "Hi, how are you?" she said. "Would you like a drink?"

"Thank you," he said.

"Adib," Michelle said. "Are you okay talking to me even though I'm a woman?"

"That is fine," he said.

"Where are you from?" Michelle knew the answer but wanted to make small talk.

Adib wanted to skip the chitchat. "Why don't you tell me why your government has detained a reporter?" he asked.

"Well, Adib, I'm afraid I don't really have all those answers right now. What I can tell you is that it is undoubtedly in your best interest to answer my questions. If you cooperate with us, it will greatly improve your chances of getting out of here."

"What kind of questions do you want me to answer today?" he said.

"I need you to explain to me your role in financing the fighters in the area where you've been working."

"Is that why I'm here?" Adib asked with either genuine or well-feigned incredulity. "I have never financed them. I will be of no help to you."

Michelle had a set of specific questions prepared on the topic, but she decided to go wide instead. "Why don't you just tell what you know, then, as a journalist, about how they are financed?"

For the next forty-five minutes Adib and Michelle carried on a genuine exchange about how certain Islamic charities help the people of that region, and how sometimes the money makes it into the hands of fighters. He dismissed as inaccurate the assertions about his own involvement with specific organizations. She didn't get any groundbreaking information out of him, but she'd gotten him talking. At least she was in on the ground floor. Before she ended the interrogation, she asked him one last question.

"Adib, how have you been treated since you've been in American custody?" she asked.

"I have lost a great deal of respect for Americans since I've been held," he said. "I am astonished at the guards' complete disrespect for our religion. And I don't think I'm the only innocent man here."

"I'm sorry to hear that," Michelle said. "Let me ask you this: when you leave this place, will you do a story on your time here? And if you do, what will it say?"

"I can't wait to do the story," Adib answered. "I'm going to tell exactly what I've seen here—that the American authorities have no respect for Islam, and they are holding innocent men without charging them with anything."

"I'm sorry you feel that way, Adib," Michelle said. "Thank you for being so cooperative today." She called the MPs to take him back to his cell.

I discovered, around this time, that the OGA had another incentive they could offer detainees who were extremely helpful, besides the comfy couch, cigarettes, treats from McDonald's, and so forth. There was a trailer that was called, by those who had reason to know, the Love Shack. I was never in an interrogation where the Love Shack was dangled as an incentive, but captives who were rewarded with special trips there got not only all the other perks, they got access to good old-fashioned porn videos and magazines as a bonus—as well as the privacy with which to enjoy them. Some of them had never seen this kind of racy material.

Reentering the world of Ben and some of the other MI interrogators required a kind of shape shifting. I worked with

Mike, an army E-5 like me, one night around 2100 when he was interrogating a Yemeni about whether he knew an individual who was believed to be connected to Al Qaeda. The Yemeni had been unresponsive in his previous sessions. We walked into the booth and Mike said, "Mohammed, are you going to cooperate tonight?"

Silence.

"Mo, why don't you want to talk to us? Aren't you sick of these games?"

Blank stare.

"Mo, I can help you if you will only cooperate."

Mohammed spoke, only to say, "Your guards have no respect for Islam. I have no reason to talk to you."

"We need to move past that, Mohammed," Mike said. "I need you to cooperate with me. Did you know Fareed Mahmoud?

Silence.

We played that game for about a half an hour, with Mohammed hunched over in his orange suit, shackled to the floor and staring at the wall.

My exposure to the detainees on the blocks had taught me that in order to make any headway with them, you had to have a firm grasp on their religious views. Many detainees had arrived as fervent believers; most of the rest had turned in that direction with their imprisonment. On a practical level, religious discussions enhanced the possibility that a detainee would let his guard down and reveal his true feelings about jihad, which was crucial to getting anywhere on the terrorism front.

I worked sessions where the interrogator seemed not to have the slightest understanding of the strange world of the blocks that these guys had been living in for more than a year: that they had teachers and encouragers waiting for them back in those cells to tell them, "You must stay strong brother; your reward is yet to come"; that they were visited by jinnis—evil spirits—and feared those more than any of the interrogator's tough talk or clever engagement. The detainees had no reason, other than blind and desperate hope, to believe that they'd be released if they started talking, and they had a great deal of incentive back on the blocks not to talk.

Too many interrogations reminded me of the prerecorded psych tech rounds on the cellblocks and the absurd drill of the detainees' responses: "I'm sleeping well; I'm eating well; I don't have nightmares; and I don't want to hurt anyone, including myself. This place is paradise."

Some of the interrogators thought they held all the aces. They knew how many of the detainees had been trying to kill themselves; they knew how miserable their lives on the blocks were; they knew they missed their wives and their kids, and probably hadn't had any contact at all with them in over a year. What too many interrogators didn't seem to understand was the sustaining power of the detainees' commitment to their faith.

One night Michelle and I interviewed an especially uncooperative detainee from Syria named Hadad. Michelle introduced herself and me, said she wasn't with the military and wanted to sit and talk. "Hadad, could you tell me a little about where you grew up?"

Hadad wouldn't look at Michelle. He said to me, "Tell her it is in the file." I relayed the message.

"I know it's in the file, Hadad, but I'd like you to tell me about it yourself," she said.

"Tell her I grew up outside Damascus," he told me.

"I understand that, Hadad. I'm interested in what your city was like, what people did for a living, what people did for fun, what were the struggles that families faced."

"I would rather not talk to her about these things," Hadad said.

Michelle tried another approach.

"Hadad, I know you are a Muslim and you try to follow the straight path," she said. "I'd be really interested to hear how you came to your faith, and whether there have been moments in your life when your faith was strengthened or renewed."

Hadad's eyes widened a bit, apparently surprised at this question.

"Sir," he said to me, "I would love to talk about these things, but not with her." Devout Muslim men do not discuss religious views with women.

Michelle called a break. "Didn't you tell me that you went to a Christian college for a couple of years and studied theology?" she asked me. "I'd like you to take about half an hour to talk to this guy about his faith. Just pause every few minutes and tell me what you're talking about. Ask him how he came to be a committed Muslim. Ask him his beliefs about God, Muhammad, Jesus Christ, and the afterlife. Find out what makes him tick religiously."

We went back in and I pulled my chair a little closer to Hadad.

"Hadad, you mentioned that you would like to talk about your religion but not with a woman. How about if you talk with me for a while about your faith and every so often I'll tell her what we are talking about. Is that OK with you?"

He nodded.

"Why don't you start by telling me how you came to follow the straight path?" This was a term that Muslims often used to describe the point in their life when they started taking their faith more seriously.

The detainee and I talked religion nonstop for the next hour. Every five minutes or so I would turn to Michelle and tell her in English what we were saying. She would respond, "Great, keep going," and add something herself now and then. The detainee explained to me that he had been living in Syria, and neither he nor his family attended Friday prayers. "I was twenty years old and obsessed with chasing girls and drinking," he said. One day he was paid a call by two missionaries from an organization called Jamiat Al-Tabligh. They told him his life was unacceptable to God. " 'Fear Judgment Day,' they said. I was afraid. I was scared that some day I would have to answer to God for my actions. So I decided to commit my life to God and serve Him only."

Then Hadad asked me about my own religion. When he found out I was a Christian, he asked me if I had read the Bible. "Yes, I've studied it quite a bit," I replied.

"Did you know that Muslims, like Christians, believe that Jesus will return to earth some day?" he asked.

"I didn't know that." I said.

"I greatly respect Christians and Jesus," he said. "But there is only one God."

"Do you believe Christians are the infidel?" I asked.

"Well, that depends." Hadad launched into a long explanation of how devout Muslims respect other "people of the book." "Whether or not someone is an infidel is dependent on the individual," he said.

"Do you believe that God loves each person?" I asked.

"I can't know this for sure," Hadad said. "I try to follow the straight path and live according to God's will. Do you believe that?"

"Well, yes. Christians believe that God loves every individual," I responded.

Hadad appeared puzzled but intrigued.

Some interrogators would have viewed that session as a waste of time, if not wildly annoying. No so-called "intelligence" had come out of it. But by getting him to understand us a little more, he trusted us more too. He talked much more freely—and productively—with Michelle in later conversations.

The tensions of the camp seemed to be wearing away more and more at everyone. Ritualistic security measures were sacrosanct, especially among the MPs, who had worst-case scenarios pounded into them from on high, but they were becoming extreme. One hot afternoon as I entered the first gate on my way back into the camp I went through the normal routine of holding up my Gitmo ID for inspection. I absent-mindedly lowered it, thinking the MP had already cleared me, and started walking toward the next gate. "Sergeant, get back here!" the MP, who was also a sergeant, yelled. I turned to see him glaring and walked back wondering what I had done to piss this guy off. "I never saw your ID," he snarled. "You are not to pass by until I clear you, Sergeant. Is that understood?" I flashed my card again silently.

Mark's pet peeves were the four-person infantry units who pulled eight-hour shifts patrolling the dusty hills around Camp Delta. We'd sometimes cross paths with them coming or going from their rounds, sweat dripping down the camo grease on their faces, twigs and leaves attached to their helmets, forty pounds of gear on their backs. All they found were unpleasant local fauna: snakes, scorpions, lizards. Just off the beach, the coast guard's swift, twenty-five-foot turn-on-a-dime Boston whalers scanned the waters day and night, guns mounted fore and aft.

These constant patrols to check that Al Qaeda wasn't around the next corner, ready to mount a daring attack to free their brothers, struck Mark as utterly ridiculous. "Al Qaeda has no offensive intelligence apparatus whatsoever!" he'd rant. "We know that! Why are we wasting these guys' time?"

Every night at the house, I'd get an earful from Mark about the insanity of life back on the blocks. Apparently a new high-ranking Taliban arrival—there was some disagreement as to whether he was the foreign minister or the ambassador to Pakistan, and I hadn't seen his file yet—had something of an attitude problem.

"So you've heard that this high-up Taliban official is now on the island right? Today on one of my calls I had the great opportunity to talk with this scumbag," Mark said one evening.

"Nice. What happened?" I asked.

"I walked up to him and asked what I could do, and he told me that he needed to be held in better conditions," Mark said. "I told him, 'Sorry, there is nothing I can do about that. Looks like you're stuck here.' He didn't appreciate my straightforward nature. Then he said to me, 'Do you know who I am?' "

"Did you know who he was?" I asked.

"Well, once he asked that, I did," Mark said. "I got excited, you know; I realized all the things I'd love to say to that shitbag—how wonderfully backward his country was, how his people lived in squalor, how proud he could be that he had helped create one of the worst governments in modern history, how—"

"Mark, finish your story," I said.

"OK, so he asks me if I know who he is, and I say, 'I really don't care who you are. You are in an American prison now. That is all that matters.' And you can just see this bastard fill with rage. Apparently, I'd struck a chord. So then he spits at me, but only landed part of it on my BDU top, and says, 'You infidel! I want to talk to a Muslim.' I said, 'No, you can talk to me; and furthermore, I'll do my best to personally fulfill all requests for a translator that come from this block in the future, ensuring that we get to work together on a regular basis.' "

"You seemed to have enjoyed yourself, Mark."

"I certainly did. Before I left I told him, 'Sir, in America we have a song "Don't Worry, Be Happy." You really need to learn to relax. I have a feeling you are going to be here a very long time.' Then I walked away."

"So I guess you're looking forward to talking to him more in the future?" I asked.

"There were three other calls to that cell block this afternoon, and I took each one," Mark said with obvious delight. "He saw me down there, and I think he truly believes he is going to be stuck dealing with me on a regular basis. I feel like I did something good today by pissing this guy off."

The interpersonal dynamics were becoming more volcanic on the JDOG side. Mo had become so annoyed with Ahmad that he moved to a different house. With Mo gone, Captain Mansur, Chaplain Yee, and the other devout Muslims had started gathering at Ahmad's more often, and the rest of the team began referring to the house as Mecca. The animosity between Dan and Captain Mansur had gotten so bad, Mark said, that Dan had filed a complaint of religious discrimination against Mansur, claiming he was always given the worst assignments. For his part, Captain Mansur was becoming openly hostile toward some of the non-Muslims, including, sometimes, Mark. "Do you know what happens to your people in my country?" he had said to Mark during a bitter argument. Mark knew that in Sudan, Christians and other non-Muslims are routinely persecuted, even murdered.

Amid all the bad blood, though, one detainee proved to be an oddly unifying force for some members of my old team.

The suicidal Saudi schoolteacher remained comatose and had been transferred to the main base hospital, where the medical staff took up his cause. They had appealed to the Arabic-speaking linguists to take turns coming by to read and talk to him. People in comas, they said, can sometimes still hear what is said to them. Most of the team helped out. Ahmad was the most devoted visitor, but just about everyone was pulling for him.

The detainees played his absence from the cells very differently. When he was taken off to the clinic and didn't come back, the very inmates who had urged him to commit suicide started a rumor that the guards had killed him in the night. The perfect way to stir up more rage against the infidels.

Meanwhile, our *Sopranos* wannabe, Ed Pagnotti, and his day shift of MPs from the Connecticut 902nd had stepped up their harassment of the detainees. It drove Pagnotti crazy that when the 902nd went off shift, the detainees were able to convince the unit coming on to restore some of the privileges the 902nd had taken away—their cups for drinking (or flinging) water, sheets, blankets, whatever. When Pagnotti's crew next came on, they would remove them again in an increasingly absurd game of give-and-take.

Pagnotti also helped improvise a new finale for IRFs. Because the IRF teams used pepper spray during their cell-extraction operations, the MPs rationalized that the spray could get in detainees' hair, causing a skin reaction. The safest thing to do, they maintained, was to shave the heads of IRFed captives. We began to notice that the detainee in question was a special favorite, the razor might "slip" and eliminate his eyebrows as well. The missing eyebrow trick made some camp officials nervous because of the potential for the Red Cross to take note, so on occasion these detainees were slapped in a special isolation cell, hidden away from Red Cross scrutiny. The Red Cross got to see all the detainees, but not necessarily on every visit; General Miller could say that certain captives were unavailable.

It looked as though even the mock IRFs, the ones done for training, had been stepped up. According to the camp grapevine, an MP had been badly hurt playing the part of a detainee during a practice IRF. It had happened in early January, just a week or so after I had my turn playing victim. But unlike mine, Sean Baker's IRF had happened in the middle of the night, in a cell. He'd been asked to wear a detainee's orange uniform, which wasn't the norm, and apparently the IRF team wasn't told he was really a fellow soldier. The team didn't realize it until after his head had been slammed against the floor a couple of times. He was airlifted to the mainland for treatment, returning to Gitmo after four days, but he had been having regular seizures. He obviously had some kind of brain injury.

There were no more IRF training drills after that.

Interactions between the MPs and Captain Mansur and the devout Muslim linguists were also very tightly wound at this point. Pagnotti in particular resented them, and he had stirred up the MPs' distrust. With his encouragement, a few of the guards had complained to camp brass that the Muslim linguists were undercutting their authority, were too sympathetic to the detainees, and seemed to be subverting the mission.

One day Captain Mansur had made the unfortunate move of taking a detainee's side in some petty cellblock dispute with an MP right in full view and earshot of the captives. The accepted procedure, when the guards and linguists were at odds, was to take the argument off the blocks. What Captain Mansur was doing on the blocks anyway, when he was the linguists' commanding officer and not expected to do the daily dirty work, was another matter noted by the guards.

Word of Mansur's transgression spread like a prairie fire through the MP ranks. Then one day, a couple of the linguists told me, Captain Mansur actually shook hands with Mark's favorite Taliban official, a gesture the MPs equated with an act of treason.

Of course, the JIG side had its own issues. The latest twist was a growing influx of civilian interrogators hired through an army contract with the firm CACI. There didn't seem to be a terribly rigorous vetting process for these hires, judging by what we saw. The basic requirement was apparently anything that could be deemed "experience"—some of them hadn't done interrogations for many years.

Two of the interrogation teams had offices adjacent to mine in the trailer. Occasionally I used one of their unclassified computers for e-mail and was startled one day to notice a microscopic dress with a sheer top, along with some thong underwear, hanging on the back of the door. I asked one of the other interrogators about it, but he avoided my question. Yet whoever owned the clothes didn't seem to think she needed to hide them; they were there day after day.

The outfit, it turned out, belonged to one of the contract interrogators. Her team worked in the middle of the night questioning Saudis who were refusing to talk. The theory was that these men were leaning on their faith and gaining strength from that connection. Her strategy was to be sexually provocative to try to make the detainee feel impure and unworthy of going before his God in prayer and thereby gaining strength. A linguist who once accompanied her in the booth told me that she had taken off her dress during the questioning and was wearing just a bra and a thong.

Another of the contracted interrogators was a portly man in his early fifties with shaggy gray hair and a matching unkempt beard. He was a complete introvert and talked to no one, and according to the military interrogators, he had been out of the intel field for decades. There were several more we wondered about. We later found out that an army policy memo dating back to 2000, which supposedly was still in effect, barred using contractors for MI jobs like interrogation, in large part for security reasons.

The number of sketchy files I'd come across and the folly of ongoing interrogations of the kind I'd witnessed with Ben and Mike was getting harder and harder to reconcile with my view of how we should be waging our war on terror. It didn't make sense that we were still holding some of these men. We obviously had no clue what to do with them, and there they sat, growing more and more despondent, more and more of them giving up hope and trying to kill themselves, and fewer and fewer of them even being interrogated at all. We did have some bad guys, and some talkers, but from what I saw, there weren't many more than a few dozen such characters at Guantánamo. General Miller nonetheless kept up his mechanical recitations about our dealing with the worst of the worst. I knew now that his boasts about the value of what we were getting from our three-million-dollar equipment were a long-distance phone call from the truth.

What I was seeing in the files matched too well with the criticisms of the camp I'd been reading in the Early Bird, and there was a harsh disconnect between the party line fed to the press and what I was seeing day in and day out. What the camp was doing to our reputation internationally was especially troubling.

Early Bird: March 12, 2003: 8:30 A.M. EST:
Detainees Are Denied Access to U.S. Courts
By Neely Tucker
Washington Post Staff Writer
Wednesday, March 12, 2003; Page A01

A federal appeals court ruled Tuesday "that the 650 suspected terrorists and Taliban fighters held at a U.S. naval base in Guantánamo Bay, Cuba, have no legal rights in the United States and may not ask courts to review their detentions," the *Washington Post* reports . . .

The attorneys for 16 detainees—12 Kuwaitis, two Britons and two Australians—sought to force the government to explain in court why the men are being held . . .

"This is a sad day for American principles of justice and fairness, and for the judiciary that is supposed to uphold those principles," Thomas Wilner and Kristine Huskey, the D.C. attorneys for the 12 Kuwaitis, said in a statement . . .

A handful of the detainees have been released, but critics of the government's position have contended that because the war on terror may last indefinitely, it is unclear whether the prisoners will ever be let go. . . .

Early Bird: March 14, 2003, 8:30 A.M. EST:
Full article: *Washington Post,* March 14, 2003, Editorial: Watching Guantánamo, Page A26:

A three-judge panel of the U.S. Court of Appeals for the D.C. Circuit held this week that no American court has jurisdiction over the government's detention of non-Americans captured and held abroad during the war. The court is right. But the story for detainees at Guantánamo Bay, Cuba, and elsewhere can't end there. While they have no viable legal claim, some may well have compelling moral claims on American values . . .

Some being held in Cuba—as well as at the Bagram air base in Afghanistan—may not be dangerous or have useful intelligence . . . The Bush administration has so far failed to put in place procedures instilling confidence that only real enemy combatants have been detained . . .

Meanwhile, Guantánamo has had a rash of suicide attempts. It is impossible, under these circumstances, to determine whether the military is engaging in a reasonable and expeditious review or warehousing people indefinitely . . .

The dissonance between fact and claim was the dirty little open secret of the camp. Though some of us bitched about the place over beers on our back patios, for the most part, we kept our heads down like good soldiers and counted the days till we got the hell out. I knew I had to find a way to cope with my growing frustrations so they wouldn't come to a boil. I'd seen others lose their cool, and I was determined not to let that happen. One effective diversion was surfing the Web looking for engagement rings for Darcie.

She and I had grown closer while I'd been away, despite the fifteen hundred miles between us. For her birthday, desperate for some creative way to celebrate, I'd decided to send her a gift a week, from the day of her birthday until the day seven weeks later that we'd be together for my midmission leave: an anklet, a certificate for a massage, flowers, lingerie, a book, earrings, a pedicure and manicure. Despite the pressures of her teaching job, she made time to bake and mail me big batches of cookies every month—snickerdoodles, chocolate chip, Hershey's Kiss—which didn't hurt my standing with my colleagues.

The night before I left for Cuba, she sneaked a small cassette recorder and a few blank tapes into my suitcase, along with a note suggesting we record messages and send them to each other. It was a great idea, especially given the prohibitive cost of phone calls, and I couldn't wait to listen to those tapes when they arrived. She usually made them while she was in the car, and they put me right back in Washington with her. "I'm nearing the White House," she'd say. "I'm driving on Constitution Avenue." "I'm stuck in traffic on the Beltway." She'd talk on the way home from her biweekly indoor soccer games—"I scored two goals tonight," or "I played terribly!" She also talked about her third graders and the vexations of teaching in the shadow of the new standardized testing triggered by the No Child Left Behind Act. And she counted the weeks we had left until we'd see each other again. I had no doubt I wanted her in my future, and I planned to pop the question at the first good opportunity after I'd escaped to normal life again.

I figured I had two options for the rest of my assignment. I could just shut myself off and ignore everything around me—throw myself into my Internet search for a diamond and set a new goal for the bench press (although Gitmo had already pushed me to my new max, a meager 240 pounds). I knew many who were taking that approach.

The other option was to take mental notes of the camp, and try to keep an open mind. After all, there were still things in intel I hadn't been exposed to. And I did know that, to say the least, there were a few bad seeds inside the wire. Sure there might be problems with the place, but maybe in the end the good would outweigh the bad. Maybe the leadership would work out the kinks—finally get those tribunals going and release some of the men who had no business being there. Maybe I should just watch, wait, and see.

I chose the latter.

Late one afternoon toward the end of March, I received the following day's schedule via e-mail from Tim and saw that I was to work with an army interrogator named Samantha the next night. She had been on the island for nearly six months. Earlier that afternoon I had seen her walking in our building, so I found her and asked if she could fill me in on the detainee before we talked to him.

"Nothing that exciting tomorrow," she said, "we're just talking to a Saudi who sometimes likes to play games. We'll be asking him mostly about possible locations of a safe house in Kandahar. Truth is, he probably doesn't know jack shit about it, but I have to ask him anyway." Safe houses were scattered throughout Afghanistan, Pakistan, and elsewhere, refuges for Al Qaeda members on the run. They were a terrorists' underground railroad. Sam was clearly annoyed by the futility of the exercise, and seemed altogether fed up with the interrogation process. On top of that, she'd just been told that her six months on the island were being involuntarily extended. "I wouldn't care if this place weren't so fucked up," she told me.

The next night, around 2100, I returned to the camp after driving the civilian linguists back to their quarters, and Sam and I went to talk to Dhakir from Saudi Arabia. Sam told me, "I have three hours blocked off for this interrogation, but I have a feeling we'll be done before 2200." That was great news to me because I was hoping to catch the end of one of the NCAA playoff games that was on that night.

We walked into the booth together, and Dhakir was sitting in a cold metal chair, ankles and wrists all locked up. As we sat down, Sam said, "How are you tonight, Dhakir?"

"I'm fine," the Saudi answered. "How are you?"

"I'm not too bad, Dhakir," Sam answered cordially.

"Listen," she continued, "I know we've talked before and you keep telling me you don't know anything; however, we have reason to believe you are misleading us. I want you to tell me about the safe house in Kandahar."

"Listen," Dhakir said, "I have never been to this house. I don't know anyone who has. I want to help you, but I can't make things up. I've never been there." Sam continued to press him, and he spent the next half hour repeating that he didn't know anything about the house. She tested his willingness to cooperate by asking what he knew about other individuals held at the camp.

"I'll tell you anything you want to know," he responded. "Ask me anything else other than about this house I've never been to." He then readily dimed out three guys who others in the camp had already corroborated had trained with Al Qaeda. He himself admitted to training with them to fight with other mujahideen, but he claimed he only intended to fight in either Bosnia or Chechnya. He said he had no hatred for the United States, a suspicious claim that probably wouldn't have held up under close scrutiny, but that wasn't our concern that night. Sam was just out for information on the safe house, and Dhakir had none. I believed him, and I think Sam did as well.

Fortunately, Sam cut the interrogation short at 2145. As we left the interrogation trailer, she shook her head and vented. "This place sucks. Had that guy even known about this house, it wouldn't have fucking mattered. It probably hasn't been operational for the past year."

I wondered if she'd been as enthusiastic about doing interrogations when she first came as I had been when I signed on.

"God, I can't wait to get out of this place," she said as she turned and walked away. "Thanks for your help."

CHAPTER TEN

Most military personnel working inside the wire were anxious not to spend a day longer at Gitmo than necessary, but that was especially true of my cosupervisor Nadia. I was trapped in the place until June, but she was due out in mid-March. She'd been counting the days, doing her job quietly and professionally but with a head that was clearly elsewhere. We didn't talk much because she preferred to keep to herself, but it was plain she hated Gitmo and missed her husband back in Washington tremendously.

More and more interrogators and linguists had found their stays involuntarily extended, like Sam and Ahmad. I heard from Mark that Ahmad was in a very bad way, although he was still pleasant whenever we ran into each other. "Kefik ya sadiqi," he'd greet me. How are you, my friend. All the military linguists had been told by camp command that we either had to find our own replacements from our home units or plan for an indefinite stay, no matter what was on our written orders; the camp had only 46 percent of its needed linguists, the leadership said. This was possibly the most unique, nonmilitary aspect of the camp. A soldier trying to locate his or her own replacement for a deployment was unheard of.

Nadia had gotten on the case and found someone to fill her slot. Her orders were expiring, she had her outprocessing papers, she'd reserved a plane ticket, and now had just forty-eight hours to go. So when she walked into our office on her next to last day with tears in her eyes, I was startled. "What's wrong?" I asked. She was usually so contained.

"They aren't letting me leave this place," she said angrily.

"What are you talking about? Why not?"

"They didn't give specifics; they just said right now they don't have enough Arabic linguists so I have to stay until they find more." Apparently, the person she'd arranged to replace her had been assigned to a different opening.

"Did you tell them you haven't used your Arabic since the day you got here?" It was true; Nadia hadn't been in a job where she had read, spoken, or listened to the language during her entire tour.

"They didn't care. The S-2 just said that I count as a linguist for his numbers, and that's all that matters." She was talking about the officer in charge of personnel, increasingly the individual most likely to be voted off the island if we were living on reality TV.

Nadia called her dad, a retired navy officer. Unless her leadership at Gitmo gave her new written orders, he advised her, she should leave, or Fort Meade could declare her AWOL.

The next night, Friday, she called me and said, "I'm going to leave. Fuck this place. I have my ticket for tomorrow; I just need a ride to the ferry." I drove the JIG linguists' van most days.

Nadia and I hadn't worked together that long, nor were we close. But I was livid over her predicament and wanted to help.

"What time do you need to be there? The van is sitting in my driveway tonight," I replied.

"I need to go at 0600. Thanks so much," she said.

In the morning we loaded up her bags. I knew I might catch flak for aiding and abetting her escape, but I doubted anyone would find out I was involved. Nadia was the one with her ass on the line.

"I'm so pissed that the army put me in this position," she said when we got on the road. "Whatever happened to taking care of their own?"

"Are you worried about what they might say at Fort Meade?" I asked, sipping my coffee as I steered the van past the base's water desalination plant. Nadia's command back home was pissed that Gitmo's leadership had given her verbal orders to stay on the island, but probably wouldn't be happy that she had left of her own accord.

"Sure, but the bottom line is that I trust them more than I do anyone here," she answered. "Erik, don't you feel as if there's a huge political undertone to everything that's done here? It's not the army I signed up for." I just nodded. When we reached the landing, we awkwardly shook hands. "Good luck," I said. "Let me know what happens."

Nadia hadn't told Major Richards she was fleeing. When I got to the office for the Saturday shift, knowing that Nadia's plane had already taken off, I wrote my boss an e-mail saying I thought she'd left, neglecting to mention my role in the venture. Major Richards let me know, when we talked later that day, that Nadia was going to be in a hell of a lot of trouble.

Sure enough, when Nadia reported for duty back at Fort Meade, she ran into a shitstorm. Her battalion commander told her she should have obeyed the verbal orders to stay in Cuba. The Gitmo command wanted to bring her back and charge her with AWOL. Her JAG lawyer told her it was doubtful the army could or would follow through with its threat of a court-martial, but she chose to accept an administrative sanction rather than risk it. It amounted to a slap on the wrist—forty-five days of extra duty—but it would always be in her record. In our e-mail exchanges, though, she said it was all worth it to be out of Cuba.

A few weeks after Nadia left, Tim, the Russian linguist who, as the JIG team's scheduler, wasn't using his Russian, slammed into the same wall and was forced to stay. He asked for new written orders to document his continued assignment for his home unit stationed in the UK. Two months dragged by. His command in Britain called and said that without the paperwork he would be declared AWOL. Tough luck, the Gitmo S-2 said. When Tim finally got back across the ocean, his commander reamed him for not getting on a plane sooner. He was never paid his per diem for the time he was in Cuba without written orders.

This was the kind of internal policy contradiction that

makes an oxymoron of the term military intelligence. It was causing mammoth morale problems for the linguists. Their reaction to the showdown with Nadia was utter disbelief. The personnel system at Gitmo was completely broken, and we were feeling flimflammed. Volunteer for a six-month tour, or ninety days if you were air force, and wham—cancel that departure date. No good deed went unpunished.

Being unequivocally uninterested by this point in an extended sojourn at Gitmo, I had contacted my unit back at Fort Meade—a sister unit to Nadia's—as her nightmare was unfolding. We had to be on top of this situation, I said; if I didn't have a solid replacement with boots on Cuban soil two weeks before I was supposed to leave in June (we had to allow time for training), the S-2 could put the brakes on my departure for who knew how long. My commander said he understood. "Relax, this won't happen to you," he reassured me.

I wanted to believe him. I'd once heard someone at the camp say that the worst thing about Gitmo was not being able to climb in a car and drive somewhere else. Being at Delta was like sweltering in a snow globe swarming with dust and mosquitoes. I was keeping the pressures of the place in check so far, but I wasn't sure how long that would last. I had to get out of there on time.

Ironically, what was happening was that many of the camp personnel were getting a taste of the way the detainees probably felt—the uncertainty and the anxiety about whether we'd be able to leave Cuba, the sense of complete powerlessness that goes with not knowing when a really bad ordeal is going to end. Every day detainees would ask, "When am I going to leave this place?" Now Camp Delta was turning into a sort of Devil's Island for all of us.

On the other hand, while we bitched about the extensions, we all felt like ingrates for complaining. After all, we might otherwise have been joining one of the divisions about to invade Iraq. Many of us had close pals and relatives who were deploying; my brother-in-law Darin, the marine chaplain, was on his way there.

The buildup was just about complete. Half a dozen aircraft carriers, including the USS *Nimitz,* were cruising the Mediterranean and Persian Gulf within striking distance of Baghdad. Hundreds of warplanes—F117 stealths, radar-dodging B-2 bombers, and others—were poised to let loose. About 250,000 American and British troops were amassed in the region. The United States was getting nowhere with a UN Security Council resolution approving the use of force, but Congress had cooperated and the train was already way down the track. On March 17, President Bush issued an ultimatum to Saddam and his sons giving them forty-eight hours to leave the country or face war.

When Operation Iraqi Freedom began on March 20 with massive air strikes on Baghdad, I was at work. Justin, an interrogator who had been recalled by the army for this mission years after leaving the service and was none too pleased about it, was in the trailer with me. He and I kept ducking into the minuscule cubicle down the hall, which had a TV, to catch the coverage. "What do you think happens if Saddam is gone tonight?" Justin asked me.

"I don't know," I said. "I don't think this will be easy even so. There are way too many Baathists in Iraq with a vested interest in staying in power. I just don't see them giving up all that easily."

Justin agreed. "Even if there is some minimal combat, then what?" he said. "The whole postconflict process is not the military's strong suit."

We sat in silence for a few seconds and stared at the screen. "Makes the war on terror sound easy," Justin said. "I've gotta run."

Opinions on going to war in Iraq varied widely among my friends at the camp. The two Iraqi Christians on my old team, Rambo and Len, were both itching for a chance to participate in Saddam's ouster. Their families had lived through the brutality of his long reign. But they were also realists. They believed the fight would be long and extremely difficult because, as Rambo said, "as long as Iraqis feel their country is being occupied, there will be those who choose to fight the occupiers. We are a very proud people."

Dan believed the United States was on a wrongheaded empire-building crusade. He thought invading Iraq was an enormous mistake and, ever the pessimist, was certain he would end up being sent there. Sure enough, he got the word shortly after war broke out that his home unit would be going. The detainees caught wind of this and heckled him constantly. They weren't supposed to hear any news, but someone always spilled the beans; they knew the war had started almost immediately. "Rah timoot fil-Eriaq," they shouted at Dan. You will die in Iraq.

Mark and I had debated the wisdom of going into Iraq

many evenings over beers while watching the nightly news. He was outrageous. He believed that the United States should openly assert itself as an imperialist power. "Erik," he'd said to me one night, "look at the Roman Empire, for God's sake. No one around them wanted to be conquered, but once they were, their lives improved drastically. They got better roads, a better educational system, and better commerce. That is what we should do in the Middle East and Southeast Asia to get these countries to join us in the twenty-first century."

As for me, I had two big concerns about the war. One, I wondered what on earth would be the end result of a dictator-less Iraq? If we wanted the place to be truly free and independent, wasn't there a good chance that a democratic Iraq would wind up looking very similar to Iran, with the Shiites in charge of a theocracy? If the two states joined forces, it could mean big trouble. Second, I worried that our efforts there would actually detract from the war on terror. Valuable assets were leaving Afghanistan and the search for Usama in order to participate in the Iraq invasion. We needed those people on the ground pursuing real terrorists in Afghanistan and Pakistan. One thing at a time. I was also reading about the possibility that Iraq could become the next lawless safe haven for them if things didn't turn out our way; even the prospect of war had already been a powerful recruiting tool for Al Qaeda.

Mark was on an air-bridge mission when the war broke out. On the day before the bombing started, he had flown from Cuba to Incirlik Air Base in Turkey with Ishtaq, a Pakistani American Urdu speaker and army reservist, and a group of MPs selected for the assignment. They overnighted there, and when they tried to take off for Afghanistan the next day, the Turks, who didn't want the United States to use their country as a staging ground for the war, held up the flight for about thirty-six hours. Finally, the green light came and the group got to Bagram and loaded up the detainees amid worried reports of incoming fire.

The flight back was more than twenty-five hours nonstop with midair refueling and the nervous edge that came with knowing the United States was at war. The bound and sensory-deprived detainees were given apples, Mark told us later, but had to attempt to eat them while blinded with blackened goggles and handcuffed with mittens on. They had no idea what they'd been handed, or even that it was food. Mark and Ishtaq tried to tell them. But since a number of them were Pashto speakers, a language neither Mark nor Ishtaq knew, they simply didn't eat. As soon as they arrived, the detainees were put through the usual rigors—kneeling in a rocky courtyard in the Cuban sun with their backs ramrod straight, being processed one by one through medical exams, cavity searches, showers, photos and fingerprinting, donning their first orange prison garb, and being hauled off to interrogation booths.

Two days after Mark's flight had left Guantánamo to retrieve the new detainees, another plane left the base, this one with detainees already aboard—eighteen Afghanis who'd been at Delta for many months and were now being sent home to freedom. This was the first group of detainees to be released since I had arrived, and only the second overall, after the four who had left in October. The government had finally determined that they weren't enemy combatants after all.

Maybe I should have been heartened by their release—at least we were admitting that these guys shouldn't have been held. On the other hand, they had been locked up all that time for no good reason, and I knew there were many more like them. Reportedly they were given no apologies upon their release and no money to compensate them for the loss of a year of their lives or to help get them on their way again.

At a party a week earlier I had talked with a couple of interrogators who were complaining about the disconnect between their ground-view assessments of the intel value of the captives and the party line in Washington. They explained to me that when they had what they considered to be a complete file on a detainee—with an appraisal that he should be released because there was no more to be gained from him (if there had been anything to start with), and little danger he would be a threat to the United States—it went to the Gitmo leadership, which in turn forwarded it to the U.S. Southern Command in Miami. From there it went to the Pentagon. Other agencies—the Defense Intelligence Agency, the OGA, the Justice Department, and others—could weigh in along the way, but "once the file's in Washington, the decisions are all political," one of the guys grumbled. How would it look to be releasing detainees at that time? How much publicity would that generate? Would releasing too many make the Gitmo operation look bad? How would it play vis-à-vis lawsuits that had been filed demanding due process for the captives?

A couple of interrogators told me that the honchos in Washington wanted to let the detainees "trickle out" to minimize bad press. How these eighteen were chosen was a mystery. The process seemed calculating, in all the wrong ways, and cynical.

At the beginning of April, a new detention area in the camp opened up, a medium-security facility, Camp Delta's version of a college dorm. The leadership called it Camp 4 in its illogically numbered incentive system (3 gave the least privileges, 2 was a little looser, 1 was better still, and 4 was now the place to be), and it was meant for the most cooperative detainees. There the inmates could replace their orange clothes with much-preferred white and sleep communally, up to ten beds per room, on thicker mattresses and even with pillows. They got real colorful prayer rugs rather than the mats they had had in their old cells. They ate their meals outside, together, and there was plenty of opportunity to play soccer or other games in the dusty courtyard around which the sleeping quarters were built.

For most detainees at Guantánamo, Camp 4 looked pretty good, and the interrogators knew it. They'd arrange to have the MPs walk the captives past it on their way to the booths and tried to entice them with it during questioning. Even in Afghanistan, our interrogators were using pictures of it to persuade prisoners to talk—better than being sent off to foreign torturers, they were told. The only detainees who wanted no part of the new facility were the Iraqi Shiites with the fatwa hanging over their heads. They were sure that if they were transferred to Camp 4, the other inmates would kill them.

For several months now over beers on our back patio, Mark and I had been shooting the shit and debating what we thought of the camp, of invading Iraq, and assorted other weighty issues, such as when I should ask Darcie to marry me and whether Mark should take the plunge and pop the question to his girlfriend, Mara. Over the thwack of basketballs bouncing on the court just over the rise at the end of our scrubby little yard, he had also kept me up on the ludicrous doings back at JDOG, and in the last weeks, I'd noticed that his attitudes about the camp had begun to change. When we first arrived, Mark had found the camp mostly intriguing, even amusing. He started asking the detainees right away about their religious beliefs and their politics; he found them fascinating, and probably saw their humanity to a greater degree than I did. Since then, the place had taken its toll on him, and he'd hardened up. He had no special sympathy for the detainees—they'd splashed him with urine and broken into spurious riots too many times for him to care about their fate—but he was pissed that the operation was such a mess.

"Erik," he said thoughtfully one night at the beginning of April, "when you came here you seemed gung ho for this mission. So what do you think now?"

"Remember how we asked everybody that same question when we first got here, and Turk said it was fucked up?" I answered.

"Yeah, that's a given, Erik," Mark said, "but I mean how do you feel about it as a soldier?"

"I'm still working that out, Mark," I said.

"I can tell you're getting soft, Saar. You know what, though, this is war. When I got here, I definitely wondered about some of these guys, how we treated them and all that bullshit, but now I could care less. I just want to fucking go home. Their problems are too big for me to worry about. Way out of our control."

He was right about that part: things at the camp were certainly out of our control. I was about to go on my midmission leave, and all I could think about that night was how the hell, once I'd set foot in the real world again with Darcie and my family, I'd ever be able to get myself back to this place.

One of the hardest things for a soldier to accept is that life goes on without you while you're gone, and you miss so much of it. A little while earlier, I had learned that my friend Mike's mom had been diagnosed with cancer. Her funeral was on St. Patrick's Day, and I couldn't believe I wasn't there. I sent Mike an e-mail and a card—big fucking deal; this was one of my brothers.

When I disembarked at Reagan National and saw Darcie watching for me there, easy to pick out with her long, light blond hair, I could have just about broken down with joy and relief, hugging her like we were vacuum packed. Over the next few days, she headed to school in Fairfax while I spent time with my parents, who had driven down from Pennsylvania. We indulged in many a fine meal out, starting with my favorite Thai restaurant near Darcie's apartment in Adams Morgan, an urban D.C. neighborhood. They all filled me in on the various events that, despite e-mail, tapes, and those expensive phone calls, I hadn't heard about yet. Dar's roommate, Jodi, had both become engaged and passed the bar, and my mom had gotten a new car—everyone's lives had gone on just fine without me. The reality of being away is pretty humbling; you learn, almost cruelly, that you are not essential.

Everyone wanted to know, of course, what Gitmo was like, and how I was doing. I wasn't allowed to tell them much, and beyond that, I was struck a bit dumb about it. I couldn't verbalize the deep aggravations; I didn't know how to articulate them to anyone who hadn't also been immersed in the camp. Mostly I just said it wasn't quite what I'd expected and that I couldn't wait till June. Normal life was so easy to slip back into, I couldn't help but wonder if after my time was up, I'd find myself thinking of Camp Delta at all.

Darcie and I had timed my leave so it would track with her school's spring break, which started three days after I arrived. She and I headed to her parents' beach house on Seabrook Island, South Carolina, for a week alone. There I forgot completely about trying to make sense of my other strange life. We strolled around Charleston, had drinks in a rooftop bar overlooking the ocean, and ate great seafood—grilled salmon with soy-lime butter for me—at Carolina's on Exchange. We played tennis, Rollerbladed, and biked. We walked barefoot and hand in hand down the beach, sipped wine on the deck while watching for shooting stars, and gratified every physical and emotional craving for each other. We fell for each other even more deeply. Leaving her to return to Gitmo was brutal.

The really big news back on base was the arrival of Pizza Hut. The place was jammed from the start. When Mark and I tried to order for delivery one night, they told us they couldn't do it. We said we'd pick up instead. "No, you don't understand," said the guy on the phone. "We're out of pizza."

In late April we went on VIP alert again. This time Major General Keith Alexander was coming through. He was the commander of the army's Intelligence and Security Command (INSCOM) at Fort Belvoir, Virginia, and because Mark and I were both part of INSCOM, along with some other intel personnel at Guantánamo Bay, he was our big boss.

Still following the usual script, General Miller brought him over to our audio communications office, crowing about the great stuff we were producing. General Alexander was tall, with thinning gray hair and nerdy glasses, heavily starched and pressed BDUs and boots shined to a perfect gloss. He looked the part of an intel guy, not a typical army officer. He didn't talk much, but it was clear that he was extremely bright.

I gave him a quick rundown of what we did, highlighting the positive to the extent I could, per the drill, but then General Alexander asked me a pointed question. How many of a certain kind of classified report had we sent out from my office?

He caught me off guard because I knew he was referring to reports released throughout the U.S. intelligence community worldwide. Our office, for all the intrigue General Miller liked to cloak it in, didn't do that. Frankly, the results of our work didn't merit that treatment. "Well, sir," I said. "We haven't issued any reports like that. Primarily our product is used internally here at Camp Delta."

He stared at me blankly and seemed to wonder what General Miller was trying to sell him.

A few other INSCOM soldiers and I were scheduled to have lunch with the general at the nearby base dining facility. I got there early and went through the chow line. There were place cards on the table for the VIPs, but not for the rest of us. A captain, once he made sure I wasn't a party crasher, barked at me, "Sit here"—directly across and one over from General Alexander's designated spot. Naturally, the general came and sat down while my mouth was full and no one else had yet arrived. "Sergeant Saar," he said, reading my name tag, "where are you from?"

"Clarks Summit, Pennsylvania, sir, but my duty station is Fort Meade."

"Is your family still in Pennsylvania?"

"Yes, sir."

"What's your MOS?" he asked, referring to my military occupation specialty.

"I'm a 98 Gulf, sir, an Arabic linguist." Linguists are all 98 Gulfs in the army's classification system. At this point two other soldiers finally sat down to my left; one officer joined us to my right.

"So what do you think of this place, Sergeant Saar?"

Here was a chance to tell him what I really thought, my big moment to spill about the place and tell him I'd come to Guantánamo eager to help defeat the terrorists but had grown more disillusioned every day, that the intelligence we were gathering was minimal at best, that if he looked in the garbage can there in the corner he might find the Geneva Conventions, that the whole operation was ill considered and a stain on our democracy.

My cojones shriveled approximately as fast as if I'd knocked a brimming pitcher of ice water into my lap. "Sir," I said, "I think we could do many things a bit differently here, but overall it's not that bad." Right, not that bad. What a goddamn lame, pansy-ass answer.

Just then a warrant officer who was working as an interrogator, seated just to my right, realized he was facing a matchless opportunity for career advancement and thought he'd get the general's ear. "Sir, I think this operation is the tip of the spear in the war on terror," he said effusively.

The general looked over, humored him for a few moments, and then turned back to me. I wasn't off the hook. "So Sergeant Saar, what exactly do you think should be done differently here?" he asked.

I told him the army hadn't trained either the linguists or the interrogators to effectively execute the mission. "At DLI," I said, "the basic Arabic course teaches you reading and listening. Here we are just about useless unless we can speak fluently, and most nonnative linguists are struggling. The native linguists have no intelligence training. Also, sir, the interrogators here are great soldiers, but they weren't trained to interrogate radical Islamists or any Arabs for that matter. They were trained to interrogate enemy prisoners of war in Eastern Europe. I think the army needs to consider adjusting fire in its training to better prepare soldiers for these realities. And sir, there are some policies at Camp Delta that are points of contention, and it would be great if they could be cleared up." Points of contention. How had I come up with that? And hell, why not mention that the marine cooks I lived with were a bunch of slobs and the phone service monopoly was a ripoff? He'd asked me a direct question. I wished I'd given him a more direct answer.

Before General Alexander could respond, his aide stepped over to tell him their next meeting was about to start.

Later that day Major Richards took him on a tour of the rest of the camp. Because Mark was also in INSCOM, she made sure that he had a quick chance to meet his boss. When the general asked him what he thought of his assignment, Fearless Mark plowed right ahead. He had left a high priority mission in the UK, he said, where he was using state-of-the-art technology to track terrorist suspects in Afghanistan, to come to Cuba, where he found himself translating for detainees wanting headache medicine and bitching about the guards.

"Sir," he said, "my mission here has no intelligence value whatsoever. Furthermore, my job here is to speak the Arabic language, but the training I received was completely focused on listening to and reading the language. I was ill prepared for this mission." Mark talks fast, so he got a lot out before Major Richards cut in. "Sir, what Sergeant Rivers is trying to say is—" But General Alexander interrupted. "Sergeant Rivers can speak for himself, Major."

Once other officers on the base found out about Mark's exercise of free speech, they weren't at all pleased, we learned. Mark had broken with the program with a VIP, a major transgression. Everyone knew there were all kinds of problems with the camp, but they sure as hell weren't supposed to be relayed to visiting brass by an impudent low-ranking NCO.

Mark's frustrations would build even higher in the coming days. The tensions on the JDOG team were taking an even more serious turn. Captain Mansur, fed up with what he perceived as disrespectful treatment of Muslims, openly accused the others of "modern-day McCarthyism." Mark filed his own religious discrimination complaint. He'd been working the solo night shift, which he loved because there were very few calls for linguists and very little rioting. The night linguist rarely got water or human waste thrown on him, and as Mark used to say, "I am all about not wearing other people's feces." Those seemed like pretty good words to live by, maybe as much of a credo as you could hope for down there. But at one point, the interrogators told the night shift MPs and linguist to start moving certain detainees to different cells each night to interrupt their sleep and keep them off balance. Mark wasn't allowed to help. It all went back to the Koran issue: he wasn't Muslim and, according to Chaplain Yee and Captain Mansur, couldn't touch the captives' Korans. Over his protestations, he was removed from the night shift.

Grievances over disparate treatment would prove to be the least of the unit's worries, though. Counterintelligence personnel started poking around the JDOG office, taking a few members of the team aside and asking them to call if they noticed anything suspicious.

A detainee told one member of the team that one of the Muslim linguists had a camera inside the wire, which was strictly forbidden. Some MPs also claimed they'd seen detainees giving letters to some of the Muslim linguists. Some of the guards' calls to the office said detainees were asking for Captain Mansur by name, which was odd since he usually didn't go to the blocks. It might not add up to much, maybe nothing at all, but in the jittery enclosure of Camp Delta it was hard to keep things in perspective.

One night when Mark was still on the late shift, a group of

counterintel guys paid a visit and asked him to open the trailer where Captain Mansur and Petty Officer Fawzi Najib, Mansur's new NCOIC and another devout Muslim, had their offices; DOCEX was there too, where Ahmad worked sometimes. The investigators said they wanted to do a shakedown. They went through the offices, checking drawers and letters and disks and Web servers. It was unorthodox for them to let anyone know they were doing a search.

Nothing happened right away. Everybody kept working as usual. If the targets of the search had any clue it had occurred, they didn't talk about it, and Mark didn't tell the other team members about it either. But there was a strong undertow of distrust running through the team, with animosities more overheated than ever and everyone watching one another. Nobody knew how it would all play out, only that it looked like it would be serious.

Meanwhile, in a strange turn of fate, the Saudi schoolteacher in a coma woke up. His motor functions were very limited, so the medical staff started him on rehab therapy, which the linguists joined in to translate. They had him hitting colors on a mobile over his bed, and in time he was able to crudely operate a wheelchair. A sure marker of his progress was the day he said to Mark about the female medics and nurses, "These women are dressed too scantily." While he treated the linguists as friends during his early recovery period, eventually his attitude became bitter. He seemed to believe he had been beaten into his coma by the guards, and Americans were again the infidel.

CHAPTER ELEVEN

Translating interrogations could pose real conundrums. In a session with Ben I found myself puzzling over how to convey one of the many obscenities he was spewing at the latest uncooperative detainee. Ben kicked a chair in front of the guy and yelled, "You are going to rot in this place, you terrorist motherfucker!"

Motherfucker really doesn't translate into Arabic very well. As the linguist, I was left to come up with my own equivalent insult while staying in character and yelling as loud as Ben was. It was tricky. Is *son of a whore* as good as *motherfucker*? *Bastard* wouldn't cut it, I knew.

By the time Brooke popped her head into my office near closing time one evening at the end of April, I could not have been less interested in such challenges. She was an army interrogator, older than me, and she had been on the island for about four months. I had talked with her at parties and in the office, and she seemed bright and competent, but I had never worked with her in the booth.

"Can you help me out with an interrogation tonight?" she asked.

She was probably talking about a late session, and I had been looking forward to getting some sleep. I also had completely lost my eager-beaver attitude about interrogations. The curiosity factor was gone; I wasn't even surfing detainees' files anymore. I was just counting the days till I could go home, and doing everything possible to make sure a replacement was lined up for me. My good friend Geoff had agreed to do a stint on the island. I felt a little guilty about pulling him into the morass, but he was the consummate company man. I knew he could deal with it. Unfortunately, none of that would cut it as an excuse to avoid the problem presenting itself. "Okay," I said. "Who was on the schedule to help you?" I still had a faint hope I could wiggle out of this.

"Mr. Salim, but I don't think he would enjoy taking part in this one. The detainee we're going to talk to is a piece of shit and we might have to turn things up a bit," she said. Mr. Salim was in his midsixties and spoke very broken English.

In the past month I had noticed that when the military interrogators were questioning a detainee who was uncooperative, they very quickly wanted to "turn up the heat": shout, be confrontational, play the bad cop, forget building rapport. I thought it was shortsighted and likely to be ineffective. Once you cross that bridge, you can't go back to being the good cop and the captive's friend.

"What time do you need me?" I asked.

"Why don't you come back around 2300?"

"No problem. I'll take the civilian linguists back to the housing area around 2000 and that will give me some down time before heading back here. Who will we be interrogating?" I asked.

"A guy named Fareek. He's a young Saudi. Recently another intelligence agency told us he took flight lessons in the same state as one of the hijackers, and he's really clammed up ever since we confronted him about it," she said.* "I'm starting to take shit from above because he's not talking. We need to try something new tonight." At 2300 we met in a trailer adjacent to the one where the interrogation would take place. The detainee had already been in the booth, alone and in chains, for an hour; she told me to grab some coffee because she'd decided to make him sit for another hour. I jumped on an unclassified computer to write to Darcie, telling her about the rainstorm we'd had. It was only the second rain in my five months at Gitmo. The water had come down in buckets, the thunder was heart stopping, and lightning had split the darkened sky so often and for such a long time you'd swear that someone, somewhere, was exacting vengeance. It was enough to make a believer out of anybody.

---

*The Associated Press received unredacted pages of an early version of this manuscript, apparently leaked by an individual employed by the Department of Defense after the authors had submitted the material to the Pentagon for review. In the resulting story published by the Associated Press in January 2005, the captive was identified as a twenty-one-year-old Saudi who had taken flight lessons in Arizona. Hani Hanjour, one of the hijackers who plunged American Airlines Flight 77 into the Pentagon on September 11, had taken lessons at two Arizona flight schools.

I wrote some e-mails to friends and one to my mom. Shortly after midnight, Brooke came in and asked if I was ready.

"Sure, let's get this done." I said, faking as much enthusiasm as I could.

As we walked across the gravel to the interrogation trailer, she told me she thought Fareek's fellow detainees were encouraging him to resist us.

"One of the MPs told me that when he returns to the cell in the middle of the night, the detainees nearby talk to him," she said. "Then he usually spends a great deal of time praying." This seemed to happen even though he was periodically moved to different cellblocks.

"I believe the problem here is that it's too easy for him to regain strength when he returns to his cell," Brooke noted. "We've gotta find a way to break that, and I'm thinking that humiliation may be the way to go. I just need to make him feel that he absolutely must cooperate with me and has no other options. I think we should make him feel so fucking dirty that he can't go back to his cell and spend the night praying. We have to put up a barrier between him and his God."

I was not looking forward to this. We opened the door to the booth and saw the Saudi, who was wearing ankle shackles and handcuffs with an additional chain connecting all his restraints to the D ring in the floor. The chain was again intentionally made too short, forcing him to hunch over in the thoroughly uncomfortable position that I'd seen quite often by that time. Two MPs were with him. The air-conditioning was turned way up. The detainee did everything possible to avoid looking at Brooke. When his eyes caught mine, they were venomous.

Brook thanked the MPs and told them they could go, "but please stay close."

"Hi, Fareek, how are you tonight?" she said, turning to our captive. As I translated her words, Fareek stood stooped over, angrily staring at the wall. "Fareek," she said, "are you going to help us tonight? You have to be getting tired of this." He didn't respond. She calmly explained that his situation would only worsen if he didn't cooperate.

"Who sent you to take flight lessons, Fareek?" No response. "What was the plan? Fareek, you have two choices here. You can either cooperate, in which case we will sit in comfortable chairs, have a smoke together, and talk like adults, or you can stand there in chains and have no hope at all of ever leaving this place or talking to a lawyer. I am the only person who can help you, and I want to do that, but I need you to answer my questions." Fareek closed his eyes and began to pray. Brooke glanced my way and motioned toward the door. When we got to the hall, she asked the MPs to go in and have him sit on a folding metal chair but remain chained to the floor. Brooke said, "Erik, I'm going to work on making him feel like he can't pray."

We returned to the booth. Brooke and I were both in our sanitized (our names were taped over) BDUs. To my surprise, she started to unbutton her top slowly, teasingly, almost like a stripper, revealing a skin-tight brown Army T-shirt stretching over her chest.

Fareek wouldn't look at her. "What is the matter, Fareek?

Don't you like women?" As she said this, she stood in front of him and tried to make him look at her body. She walked slowly behind him and began rubbing her breasts against his back. "Do you like these big American tits, Fareek?" she said. "I can see that you are starting to get hard. How do you think Allah feels about that?" The detainee was visibly bothered but still didn't speak. She moved in front of him and took a seat. "What do you think, Fareek?" she said, placing her hands on her breasts. "Don't you like these big tits?" He glanced, saw what she was doing, and immediately looked away.

"Are you gay? Why do you keep looking at him?" Brooke asked, referring to me. "He thinks I have great tits! Don't you?" Caught off guard, I just nodded as I kept translating, which had gotten uncomfortable enough for me; I didn't want to be drawn in further. "This is all your choice, Fareek, we can go on like this all night or you can start to answer my questions," she said. "Who sent you to flight school?"

Fareek was beginning to shake and his face was filled with intense loathing. He looked my way and our eyes locked for a good ten seconds. I wanted to look intimidating, but I wondered if he could sense my own doubts about what was taking place.

I was sure Brooke didn't think she was out of line, and I doubted anyone in the leadership would have thought so either. It was understood that it was within bounds to place enormous mental and spiritual pressure on detainees. Although it was possible for supervisors to observe interrogations through the one-way glass in each room, they rarely did so, and we would have been able to hear if someone came into the creaky trailer to watch. There were also cameras in the booths, but the sessions were not recorded; General Miller thought taping could only cause legal problems. The video was simply fed to a screen in the observation room. For the overwhelming majority of sessions, the only ones who ever knew what took place in the booth were the interrogator, the linguist, and the detainee. But in any case, if we felt queasy about what was happening, it wasn't because we thought we were breaking any rules. That Geneva Convention meeting had blurred all the lines.

I had never in my life felt such concrete emotion coming from someone's eyes. It wasn't just hatred. It was a look that communicated violence. I was completely confident that this man would kill us if he had the opportunity. I hoped that we would learn how he got to flight school in the United States, but I was skeptical. And this approach trespassed on sacred ground, so I wasn't feeling so great about myself at the moment.

After we broke our gaze, the detainee responded to Brooke's question by looking up and spitting in her face. She was unfazed and didn't budge. "I see how it is," she said. "Just remember, you have the power to make this stop."

Then she and I again left the room. She told the MPs to stand close by; she might need them in the next round. We walked down the hall to talk to Adel, another linguist who was getting ready for a different interrogation. Brooke asked this Muslim for advice.

She had a high-priority uncooperative detainee, she explained, and she wanted to find a way to break him from his reliance on God, his source of strength. He suggested that she tell the Saudi that she was having her period and then touch him. That could make him feel too dirty and ashamed to go before God later, he said, adding that she should have the MPs turn off his water so he couldn't wash later.

I thought it was odd that a devout Muslim would suggest this treatment for a fellow believer, but Brooke seized Adel's idea and built on it. She grabbed a red marker and disappeared into the ladies' room. "Let's go," she said when she returned. Before we entered, she warned the MPs again to stay close by and come in if they heard any screaming.

We sat across from the detainee. "Fareek, is Islam a violent religion?" she asked.

No response.

"Do you know that innocent Muslims died in New York City on September 11? Do you really think this pleases your God?" Brooke's tone was scornful. "Who sent you to take flight lessons?" Fareek was completely unresponsive and refused to look at her. She said, "Do you really think your actions in here are pleasing to Allah? How do you think he feels about your being attracted to this infidel American woman?"

As she said this, she stood and moved her chair out of the way. She started unbuttoning her BDU pants. "Fareek, did you know that I'm having my period?" she said. She placed her hands in her pants as she started to circle behind the detainee. "How do you feel about me touching you now?"

Fareek's spine shot straight as a steel rod. As I translated, he looked at me as if my death was his most profound desire.

Brooke came back around his other side, and he could see that she was beginning to withdraw her hand from her pants.

As it became visible, the Saudi saw what looked like red blood on her hand. "Who told you to learn to fly, Fareek?" she demanded. He glared at her with vengeance, refusing to give in. "You fuck," she hissed, wiping what he believed was menstrual blood on his face.

"Aaaaaaaaaaaaaaahhhhhhhhhhh!" Fareek was screaming at the top of his lungs, rattling the flimsy trailer, body shaking, beginning to sob. He kept yanking his arms apart, as if he could somehow wrest himself out of his handcuffs.

"How do you like this?" she asked, holding open the palm of her hand to show him her blood.

Fareek spit at both of us and shouted again, this time a more pleading, fearful cry. His voice quivered as he screamed, and he lunged forward out of his chair, breaking loose from one of his ankle shackles. He began to scream, wail, and shout, "La la la." No no no.

"What the fuck are we doing?" I said to myself.

The MPs rushed into the room and Brooke said to the lower-ranking one, "Fix the fucking shackles, leave him lying on the floor, and get the fuck out!" The MP did as he was told.

Brooke got down on her knees next to him. I followed suit. "It doesn't have to be this way," she said. "You have choices, Fareek. Who sent you to flight school?" He began to cry like a baby, sobbing and mumbling in Arabic too indistinct for me to understand. The only thing I picked out was, "You American whore."

"What do you think your brothers will think of you in the morning when they see an American woman's menstrual blood on your face?" Brooke said, standing up. "By the way, we've shut off the water to your cell for tonight, so the blood will still be there tomorrow," she tossed out as we left the booth.

We closed the door behind us, and I leaned against the wall. I was relieved to be out of there, and also utterly drained. Brooke looked at me and began to cry. She too was exhausted, but wholly frustrated as well.

I just looked at her. I knew she hadn't enjoyed this. She had done what she thought was best to get the information her bosses were asking for.

Had someone come to me before I left for Gitmo and told me that we would use women to sexually torment detainees in interrogations to try to sever their relationships with God, I probably would have thought that sounded fine. And if someone had spelled out for me the details of the interrogation I had just participated in, I probably would have approved.

But I hated myself when I walked out of that room, even though I was pretty sure we were talking to a piece of shit in there. I felt as if I had lost something. We lost something. We lost the high road. We cashed in our principles in the hope of obtaining a piece of information. And it didn't even fucking work.

I'm sure I must have said good-bye to Brooke. I know that I left and headed straight for the gate without another word to anyone else. It was about 0130 and I got in the van, started it, and sat for a few seconds staring at the looping concertina wire surrounding the camp.

What the fuck did I just do? What the fuck were we doing in this place?

I put the van in drive and started back toward the house. Most of America was asleep, but I was wide awake, defending freedom, honor fucking bound. There was no honor in what we had just done. We were grasping, and in doing so we had spit on Islam. Our tactics were way out of bounds. What we did was the antithesis of what the United States is supposed to be about.

I walked in the house and went straight for the phone, taking it to the tiny laundry room where I knew I wouldn't be heard. I couldn't tell Darcie anything about what had just happened, but I needed to connect. I was profoundly unnerved, saddened, shaking. After a few rings she answered with a muffled, sleepy hello. "I love you, baby," I said, faltering. I just wanted to be home with her.

"What's wrong, Erik?"

"Nothing, Dar, I just wanted to hear your voice."

"Erik, tell me what is wrong; I can hear it—your voice is trembling."

Tears were rolling down my cheeks, but I swore I wouldn't let her know I was crying. "I'm all right, baby, I just wanted to tell you I love you. I really can't tell you what's bothering me here, but I can't wait to get home. Go back to sleep, sweetheart. I love you."

I hung up and went upstairs to the bathroom, throwing my uniform on the floor and turning on the shower. There wasn't enough hot water in all of Cuba to make me feel clean. My hatred for that godforsaken fucking place seemed to condense into a hard ball in my chest. I sat down in our filthy tub and let the hot water hit my head and the steam thicken the air as

I cried. I sat there for half an hour. When I finally lay down in bed, I just stared at the ceiling. Sleep kept being chased away by shame.

I went downstairs at 0600, fried and looking for some coffee. I would have killed for Starbucks. During the next week I asked Tim not to schedule me for any more interrogations.

On May 1, President Bush stood on an aircraft carrier with a big banner hung behind him declaring MISSION ACCOMPLISHED. He announced the end of major combat operations in Iraq. I watched it on the news that night, thinking that it couldn't really be that easy. Overall, though, the feeling on the base seemed to be right in line with the macho image projected by the banner and our commander in chief in his flight suit.

That month two more flights left the island carrying a total of eighteen detainees home. But another one arrived bringing new captives; I wasn't sure how many were on board, but I heard there was a net gain. My scans of the Internet turned up articles about a stern letter that Secretary of State Powell had written Rumsfeld about Gitmo. Some detainees clearly needed to be released, he said, and he cited complaints from eight allies who wanted their citizens back. He also made the point that the military's mishandling of Guantánamo and the "enemy combatant" problem had undermined America's ability to enlist its friends to help fight the war on terror. Rumsfeld fought back but the upshot, it was reported, was that the Pentagon would expedite the transfer of a hundred or more detainees to their home countries. We'd see if that happened.

Every ten days or two weeks since Nadia had left, I had received an e-mail from Major Richards or from my command at Fort Meade warning me not to get on a plane and leave if I was verbally ordered to stay, as she had. But I had worked assiduously with my home unit to make sure I wasn't stuck there past my June 6 departure date. My buddy Geoff was supposed to be on his way. Unbelievably—or maybe not—despite all my efforts, there was some kind of paperwork holdup, and I got the order to stay.

I went a little nuts. I called everyone I could think of who might get things back on track. I wrote my entire chain of command, describing not just my problem but how the broken personnel system contributed to the rock-bottom morale on the base. Since my official residence was still in Pennsylvania, I wrote my congressman, Paul Kanjorski, and one of my senators, Rick Santorum. But the thing that worked was my e-mail to General Alexander, who had been through Gitmo in April and was at the top of my command. He wrote me back within an hour saying he'd get to the bottom of it. Sure enough, the paperwork got fixed and I felt a huge weight fall away.

When Geoff, who was an extremely disciplined soldier, moved in with us, he was a little startled at how pathetically filthy the house was. Mark was the highest-ranking guy living there and could have ordered everyone to clean up, but sanitation just wasn't one of his priorities. He was never your typical soldier. I tried to convince Geoff of the pleasures of relaxing on broken furniture with seven other guys fighting over a remote in a living room with a cold tile floor covered in a quarter inch of dirt, and I reminded him that he could be in open-bay housing.

Once Geoff was corporeally in Cuba, Major Richards cleared me to reserve a seat on the June 20 flight to Jacksonville—only fourteen days past my scheduled departure, which was nothing in army time. I began packing six months' worth of stuff and couldn't wait to lug those bags to the leeward side of the island. I showed Geoff how things were run in my office. At his first Saturday meeting, I introduced him to the civilian linguists he'd be supervising and they welcomed him with open arms, as they had me. Geoff had always had a positive attitude, and I knew he'd make up his own mind about the camp. I tried not to convey my disillusionment, but it wasn't easy.

Although I was itching to leave, I knew I wasn't going to be anyone's favorite soldier at Fort Meade when I reported for duty. I had rocked the boat with my e-mail to General Alexander, and my first sergeant sent an e-mail accusing me of being disloyal to my unit. I didn't know if I wanted to confront him and my commander and tell them they were hanging the soldiers they sent to the chaotic mess of Gitmo out to dry, or just take my licks and keep my head low for my final year in the army.

Mark was in the middle of dealing with his own home unit about getting out of Gitmo. He and I had arrived on the same day; we should have been leaving at the same time as well. But his unit didn't want to send a replacement, so they were working on other ways of getting him out. He was jealous when he saw me packing.

Before I left, I had one more conversation with Mustapha, the Syrian detainee with whom I'd had long talks about religion when I was on the JDOG team. I told him I was going. "Mustapha, we've talked a lot over the past six months, and we've learned a lot about each other," I said. "I have one last question. I want to know what you think of me."

Sitting cross-legged on the floor as usual, Mustapha smiled and gazed down the corridor of Echo block, taking in the atmosphere and the breeze coming off the ocean he couldn't see. "Basam," he said. "You are not how I thought an American man or soldier would be. You believe in God and you love your family. In a way I respect you. But you are a kafer"—an infidel. "You are not a Muslim. In fact, you are an enemy of the true God. If I were not in this cell I would have to kill you."

I wasn't totally surprised by his answer. He had a curious mind, but I knew he was committed to Islam. Still, it was a sobering reminder of what enormous challenges lay ahead in trying to change the views of the multitudes like him who hated Americans. And at Gitmo we'd set a precedent that would only make the hatred worse.

Mark managed to get possession of the JDOG van and took me to the ferry landing at 0630 on Saturday. I got my bags out of the back and wished him good luck getting out of Gitmo, giving him a guy's standard half hug with a few heartfelt pats on the back. "Take care, bro', good luck with that girl of yours," he said.

"Same to you," I told him.

From the ferry I watched the finale of a spectacular sunrise—another chance to ponder Gitmo's many contradictions. There weren't many people on board. It was obvious that there were more people arriving on the island than leaving, and I had been noticing a lot of construction in the past few months. From all appearances, Camp Delta was going to be there for the long haul.

On the leeward side, I caught a neon-orange school bus up to the airport with my enormous suitcase, garment bag, and two duffels. The MPs checked my ID and orders. I was lucky enough to get a window seat on the Continental jet, and my stomach did a satisfied flip as I felt the wheels start to move. We took off, and I stared one final time at the island below.

From Jacksonville I caught a US Air flight to Philly. Darcie and I became one of those couples you see making out in the airport as if nobody else exists. We were headed straight to Avalon; it was the weekend of the annual gathering of our very good friends, where a year earlier Darcie and I had recognized our mutual attraction. As we walked to baggage claim I noticed another couple kissing with tears in their eyes; they were saying their good-byes. I squeezed Dar's hand.

When we walked through the door of the beach house after an hour's drive, Timmy's six-foot-one 250-pound frame encased me in a bear hug. Swelly handed me an ice-cold

Yuengling Lager, our beer of choice when we gathered at home. Dar had made a cake: "Welcome Home Erik." We all celebrated for a few minutes, then I grabbed Mike and took him out to the deck. I hadn't talked to him since his mother had lost her battle with cancer, and I told him how much I wished I had been able to be there for him during his worst hours. We hugged and he told me he was hanging in there.

That night about twenty of my closest friends and I danced until well past 2:00 A.M. at an Avalon bar, the Princeton. It was good to be home.

My command had given me Monday off, but I had to report to Fort Meade on Tuesday morning. Within five minutes I'd been called into the office of Major Talbot, the head of our battalion's S-3 office, which was responsible for sending soldiers on deployment. He and Captain Harris, my company commander, gave me the lecture of my military career. They told me my contact with General Alexander was "deplorable," accused me of having no regard for my own chain of command, called me disloyal. I tried to explain the poisonous state of affairs at Guantánamo, but they didn't want to hear it. They were more concerned with the fact that I had made them look bad. A few months later, I wrote about some of my Gitmo concerns in a Command Climate Survey, a periodic evaluation we all did of our leadership. I wrote about the mismanagement, the upside-down security situation, the broken personnel structure, and morale problems. Nobody ever asked to speak with me about my experience.

Mark, meanwhile, didn't get out of Cuba until August, more than two months after his promised departure date. Geoff, my replacement, was kept there without orders well into 2004, three months after he'd been told he could leave.

And at that time, more than six hundred men were still awaiting their fates at Guantánamo.

Epilogue

In July 2003, just a month after I'd arrived home, Guantá-namo was all over the news. On July 3, President Bush fi-nally declared six detainees eligible for trial by military commissions, including two from the UK and an Australian. The development brought a fresh slew of worldwide critiques of Gitmo, with the British press leading the way. On July 17, President Bush met with British Prime Minister Tony Blair to try to work out Blair's concerns about the trials of the two Brits. At a joint news conference, Bush responded to a question about the open-ended imprisonment of the detainees in Cuba: "The only thing I know for certain is that these are bad peo-ple." Near the end of the month, a congressional delegation left for Cuba to tour the detention camp.

I had mixed reactions to these events: hope that the com-missions would finally get rolling and either convict or exon-erate the detainees; resignation to yet more condemnation from our friends abroad; dismay that Bush was again publicly prejudging the guilt of every one of the detainees. And I could only shake my head about the visit by the congressional delegation; I had no doubt Gitmo officials had spent weeks touching up the façade they'd present to these VIPs.

On September 10, Guantánamo Chaplain James Yee was arrested when he arrived in Florida for a short leave; the Pentagon didn't announce it until ten days later. Yee was told he'd be charged with sedition, mutiny, spying, and aiding the enemy, and he was held in solitary for seventy-six days. On September 23, military officials announced that my JDOG colleague Ahmad al Halabi had been arrested exactly three months earlier when he arrived in Jacksonville. It happened as he left Gitmo after serving two involuntary extensions and just a few days before his scheduled wedding in Syria. He was charged with espionage and a host of other serious offenses, and he faced the death penalty. Ahmed Mehalba, one of the civilian linguists I supervised in my JIG office who had worked some interrogations with the contract interrogator with the suggestive clothing, was arrested September 29 at Logan Airport in Boston, where he'd just arrived after visiting his father in Cairo. He was accused of having illegal possession of classified material that was on a CD in his bags. He, too, was thrown in jail for months. Unnamed military sources talked of a possible spy ring, suggesting that these three may have been linked in a plan to help Al Qaeda or Syria obtain classified information about the detention operation and messages from the detainees. It was all very vague, but the media was having a field day. I knew that several other Gitmo personnel were being investigated as well.

There's no doubt in my mind that the bad blood between the Muslims and non-Muslims working at the base contributed to the arrests. Small incidents were inflated and misunderstood. A climate had been created at Gitmo that made it all too easy. Ultimately, what they went through was a lot like what the detainees have had to endure: presumptive guilt and imprisonment based on suspicion rather than proof.

In the end, Chaplain Yee was charged with far lesser offenses, like mishandling classified information. As investigators dug into his life, they added on the unconnected charges of adultery—a punishable offense in the military—and keeping pornography on a government computer. The criminal charges were dropped; it turned out that the material he had with him was not classified. Had the security regime at Camp Delta been less paranoid and more well thought out, that should have been clear to begin with. He was found guilty of the noncriminal adultery and porn charges after prosecutors put a woman on the stand to give lengthy testimony, as his wife watched in agony, about her intimate relationship with the chaplain. He received a reprimand, but even that was thrown out a month later.

The case against Ahmad crumbled in similar fashion. Using his own laptop to translate detainee letters had come back to haunt him, as some of the thirty-two crimes he was charged with were linked to the fact that many of those letters were still on his computer and were considered classified. He spent ten months in jail while he awaited trial. But then, as in the Yee case, the government acknowledged that the material wasn't classified after all. One of the other charges against Ahmad, aiding the enemy, was based on an allegation that he gave baklava to the detainees. It evaporated when Ahmad's legal team showed that he hadn't even been on base at the time—he was on the air-bridge mission that the JDOG team had so much resented him being picked for. In fact, there was no basis to substantiate most of the charges, and in late 2004 he cut a deal on the few that remained—taking two photos of a guard tower, for instance, even though the media and others had done the same. He was sentenced to the ten months he'd already served.

Ahmed Mehalba, the civilian, pleaded guilty on January 10, 2005, to a single count of mishandling classified information for carrying the computer disk on the air-bridge trip to Egypt, and two counts of making false statements.

I knew all of these men. I had no knowledge of what they did or didn't do in connection with the charges. There was no doubt that information was overclassified regularly at Gitmo, and that classified material is "mishandled" all the time, in the sense that it's not treated according to every last letter of the law. Unfortunately, it's the wrong time in our history to be called on that breach.

And I can say unequivocally that the chaplain and the linguists were placed in a terrible situation. Their religious convictions put their actions under a microscope and led to conclusions—such as the mistaken assumption that the base had been penetrated by jihadists or a hostile government—that weren't tethered to reality. When a white non-Muslim colonel, Jack Farr, was charged in November 2003 with transporting classified information without the proper container (technically classified papers are supposed to be carried in a locked case) and making a false statement to investigators, he wasn't put behind bars. His charges were settled with administrative punishment, and almost no specifics were made public. Each case is different, but I had to wonder if things would have been handled the same way if he'd been lower ranking and a staunch follower of Islam.

What hasn't come out in any of these investigations is an assessment of the leadership's responsibility for the events that transpired at Gitmo. One of the core lessons you learn in the army, starting in basic training, is that excuses are not tolerated. I loved this lesson. Whether it's blowing a room inspection or falling out of a ruck march, when a superior asks you why you failed, you are *never* to make an excuse. Somehow, this concept seems to disappear at the rank of colonel and above. Why hasn't any leader been held accountable for the failure that is Guantánamo Bay? Why are they allowed to make all the excuses?

Why didn't anyone see how combustible the situation was? Why did the leaders allow individuals with interim clearances to have access to sensitive information? Why were people with little or no training placed face to face with alleged terrorists who shared many of their religious convictions and who would do anything to have an ally on the inside?

The government hasn't come away looking any better on the broader legal front. In June 2004, in a case called *Rasul v. Bush*, the Supreme Court reversed the appeals court that had said the detainees had no standing in federal court. Gitmo, the justices ruled, is "territory over which the United States exercises exclusive jurisdiction and control." It was a huge loss for the Bush administration's terror policy, blowing apart the whole rationale for choosing Gitmo as a holding tank. Sensing trouble coming, the Pentagon had begun expediting the release of some detainees even while the case was in the pipeline. But since the ruling, the administration has fought to interpret it narrowly, at first not even allowing lawyers to meet with the detainees until another court intervened.

Meanwhile, the Pentagon brought each detainee before an administrative panel tasked with deciding whether he should be at Gitmo—whether he is, in fact, an enemy combatant, as President Bush had originally declared all the detainees were. But the detainees weren't permitted to have attorneys present, and the government used secret evidence against them. As this book went to press, 506 detainees had been found to be enemy combatants, 33 were not and are to be released, and 19 cases had yet to be decided. The Pentagon began the reviews hoping they would satisfy the Supreme Court's concerns about due process without allowing the detainees to go to federal court. But dozens of prisoners have filed motions regardless, challenging the right of the United States to hold them so long without charges, lawyers, or trials, and most are expected to follow.

Separately, the military commissions were stopped before they ever started. A preliminary hearing for the detainee who was to be tried first, Salim Ahmed Hamdan, a former driver for Usama bin Laden, was abruptly halted in November 2004, when a federal judge in New York said it couldn't go forward because the administration had ignored the Geneva Conventions, specifically the requirement for individual reviews to determine whether captives are POWs under the law.

Against a backdrop of triple- and quadruple-tiered legal maneuvering, the International Committee of the Red Cross broke its customary public silence in October 2003, pushed to do so, it said, by a spate of suicide attempts. "One cannot keep these detainees in this pattern, this situation, indefinitely," a senior official said. By the time of the Red Cross's statement, the official number of suicide attempts was 32, though I knew it was actually far higher. The device of labeling most attempted suicides as "manipulative self-injurious behavior" kept the numbers low, and Camp Delta's command seemed to be using that designation more often. The military's count of these fake "manipulative" suicide attempts wasn't released until January 2005, when it disclosed that a mass attempt by 23 detainees had taken place in August 2003. The Pentagon said that 350 "self-harm" incidents occurred that year, including 120 "hanging gestures." It doesn't take the smarts of my rocket-scientist pal Timmy to know that it's dangerous to parse when somebody is really trying to kill himself and when he's just trying to get attention. Sometimes it's both at once.

In November 2004, the *New York Times* broke the news that the most recent Red Cross report sent to the U.S. government contained charges that the military was using coercion tactics that were "tantamount to torture" on Gitmo detainees, including exposure to extreme cold, loud noise and music, stress positions, solitary confinement, and "some beatings." It also reported that doctors and medics were helping plan for interrogations by informing the psy-ops, or Biscuit, team about the medical conditions of detainees in what the Red Cross called "a flagrant violation of medical ethics."

After a lawsuit by the American Civil Liberties Union, FBI

memos were released beginning in 2004 that laid out similar images of aggressive tactics—detainees found shackled to the floor in fetal positions for more than twenty-four hours, left without food or water, or intimidated by growling dogs. Detainees exposed to extremely loud rap music and strobe lights. A captive draped in an Israeli flag. Extreme temperatures. Sleep deprivation. One interrogator taped the curtains shut on her booth's one-way glass, then stood between the monitoring camera and the detainee she was questioning, who looked to be in pain; a marine told an FBI observer that she had squeezed the detainee's genitals and bent his thumbs backward. The memos showed that there was an ongoing dispute between the FBI and the military over interrogation methods, with the FBI leaning toward rapport building and the military on the side of harsher treatment. The memos indicated that the FBI had complained to General Miller more than once.

Woven into the building scrutiny of how we were treating our detainees was the disclosure of the Abu Ghraib prison scandal in Iraq. On April 28, 2004, CBS's *60 Minutes II* broadcast harrowing photos taken there by U.S. soldiers holding suspected insurgents for questioning. The photos shown that night, as well as those that emerged in the following days and weeks, pictured acts that went far beyond any that most Americans could imagine their soldiers committing: stacking naked prisoners in a pyramid and jumping onto them, letting growling dogs loose on naked captives, attaching wires to a hooded man and telling him he'd be electrocuted if he fell off the boxes he was standing on, making naked prisoners perform or simulate sex acts. It was a circus of horrors.

As we have all learned since the Abu Ghraib scandal was revealed, the Bush administration had been in intense internal discussions since 9/11 about the powers of the president versus the language of the Geneva Conventions. On January 9, 2002, two Justice Department lawyers advised the Pentagon that Taliban and Al Qaeda members were not protected by the Geneva Conventions. (Some of the documents mentioned here are included in an appendix that follows.) Thirteen days later, assistant attorney general Jay Bybee, who is now a federal appellate judge, wrote to White House counsel Alberto Gonzales, who is now the attorney general, making a similar argument, which Gonzales echoed in a memo to President Bush. Gonzales dismissed objections by Secretary of State Colin Powell, who had maintained that Geneva should apply. Powell argued for reconsideration of Gonzales's position, saying it would make it easier for enemy troops in any conflict to mistreat our own captured soldiers. He did not prevail. The back and forth was going on as the first detainees were arriving at Camp X-ray.

On August 1, 2002, Bybee wrote another memo to Gonzales, this time laying out his opinion of what constitutes torture under international agreements and laws. For treatment to be considered torture, Bybee wrote, "The victim must experience intense pain or suffering of the kind that is equivalent to the pain that would be associated with serious physical injury so severe that death, organ failure, or permanent damage resulting in a loss of significant body function will likely result." Bybee also said that in any case, Bush could circumvent Geneva in the name of national security.

It turned out that Secretary Rumsfeld had authorized a new set of more aggressive interrogation techniques in December 2002, the month I arrived at Gitmo, specifically in response to questions about how far interrogators could go with the supposed twentieth hijacker. When he okayed this memo, he scribbled at the bottom, "However, I stand for 8-10 hours a day. Why is standing limited to 4 hours?" That was apparently a comment on how long detainees could be forced to stand or otherwise be kept in stress positions. Rumsfeld pulled the order back about six weeks later, although he allowed use of some of the aggressive tactics on a case-by-case basis, with his approval. A final list of acceptable methods was issued in April 2003, again with some requiring assent from higher-ups.

The memos helped show how Abu Ghraib could have happened, once again illustrating the dangers of sending ambiguous signals in a stress-packed military environment. Even though Geneva did apply in Iraq, that wasn't clear to a lot of key personnel after what they'd seen of the treatment of captives in the war on terror. General Miller's visit to Abu Ghraib in the fall of 2003 to consult on how to get more info from the captives there may have further muddied the distinctions. He emphasized the importance of the MPs' "setting favorable conditions" for interrogators. I was surprised when he was sent back to Abu Ghraib after the scandal broke, this time to take charge of gathering intelligence from the eight thousand men and women we had locked up.

Given some of the stories that have now come out of Iraq, Afghanistan, and Gitmo, I no longer know what to believe when I hear a new allegation. And what went on at these various U.S.-run facilities isn't even the worst of it. The practice of rendition—sending suspects to certain countries such as Jordan and Egypt, where torture is practiced—by our main overseas intelligence agency is a phenomenally disingenuous way of keeping our hands clean. While my encounters with the OGA were positive, we now know that it's been involved in some extremely troubling incidents involving detainees in Iraq and elsewhere.

My time in Guantánamo didn't make me love my country any less. And those six months couldn't erase the overall positive experience I had in the U.S. Army, an institution filled with men and women who would sacrifice everything to protect their nation. I'm proud to have worn army green and to have served with those who belong to the generation that has been called to defeat terrorism. But what I saw, and the continuing revelations since I left that have allowed me to put it in context, convinces me that we should be a lot smarter about fighting this enemy.

To me, Gitmo represents failure on two fronts. The first failure is a moral one. Our government's dangerous dance around the Geneva Conventions and the use of questionable tactics on the detainees at Gitmo and elsewhere is morally inconsistent with what we stand for as a nation. We claim to honor the principles of justice and human rights. I didn't personally see anything that I would label torture as most people understand the word. But I saw many things that were dehumanizing, that degraded us all.

When I took the oath of enlistment along with other future soldiers back in 1998, I swore to defend and uphold the

Constitution of the United States of America. I believe that there is an inherent promise given to every soldier, sailor, airman, and marine who in turn pledges his or her life in the country's defense: The country will only use you to defend the principles embodied in that revered founding document. Guantánamo represents a broken promise. We're accurately called hypocrites when we deny any sort of justice or due process to individuals in the name of protecting America.

The second argument is more practical. The price we are paying for Gitmo is too high given the meager results we are getting. Guantánamo is a rallying cry throughout the Arab and Muslim world, and even some of our closest allies oppose us in this venture. The bottom line is this: the minimal intelligence we are gathering from those held in Cuba is not worth the harm we are doing to our international reputation. It's costing us our moral leadership in the world. How long until we pause, look over our shoulder, and find no one is following?

President Bush has warned that winning this war will take a long time. He's right; this war will last decades, not terms of office. To me, that means we need a perspective that recognizes that the tactics we use in fighting this enemy now will determine the long-term outcome. It's easy to say that we'll be safer if we round up the alleged terrorists and hold them indefinitely. But we have to act with an eye on the decades ahead. How we treat our suspected enemies—whether we respect their religious convictions and allow them a fair shot at justice—will help determine how many future terrorists we create, just as the head of the DIA, Vice Admiral Lowell E. Jacoby, told the Senate Intelligence Committee in February 2005 regarding the Iraq war: "Our policies in the Middle East fuel Islamic resentment," Jacoby said. "Overwhelming majorities in Morocco, Jordan, and Saudi Arabia believe the U.S. has a negative policy toward the Arab world."

About 200 detainees have been released or transferred to the custody of their home countries since the Guantánamo operation began; about 550 remain there now. A dozen or more of those released have been apprehended again or killed fighting the United States after they returned home, including one of the teenagers who'd been kept at Camp Iguana. One man who hasn't yet been recaptured has bragged to reporters about deceiving the Gitmo interrogators into believing he was an innocent Afghani tribesman, not a Pakistani militant. The stories show how complicated our task is. But it's amazing to me that even more aren't on the warpath after what they went through.

The military is acting as if most of the captives are there to stay. There's a new, hard-walled maximum-security prison that can hold one hundred prisoners and has special interrogation rooms. And in the works is a twenty-five-million-dollar facility that would hold as many as two hundred more. Guantánamo has turned into a long-term penal colony for suspects, almost all of them Muslims, who have never faced a judge or jury. It's our warehouse in the war on terror.

It's difficult to see how the United States, in good conscience, can hold other nations to standards we're not meeting ourselves. In a head-snapping move in February 2005, the State Department issued its annual human rights report, criticizing countries for a range of practices it called torture—including sleep deprivation, threatening prisoners with dogs, stripping them—methods we've used in our own detention camps. The report attacked treatment of prisoners in countries like Syria and Egypt, two of the nations which the OGA has used for renditions, shipping terrorism suspects there for questioning precisely because their interrogators are known for taking the gloves off.

I'm no foreign policy expert, but I know that if we as a nation build a wall of fear with the Arab and Muslim world, it's a decision with far-reaching consequences. I'm discouraged by evidence of the preconceptions that have taken root in our country since 9/11. A Cornell University poll in December 2004 found that 44 percent of Americans surveyed think that the rights of Muslim Americans should be curtailed in some way—by requiring them to register their location with the federal government, for instance. It's a long way from the mind-set we need if we're going to engage more with the Arab nations and help build better futures for their youth—actions that are not only the right things to do, but are in our interest.

My last day in the army was May 27, 2004. On June 27, Darcie and I were married on Seabrook Island, where we had spent a week in the middle of my assignment in Cuba. I worked for a few months with the FBI as a contract employee, then decided to work in the private sector doing something entirely different. I hope someday to serve my country again.

When I was on Seabrook with Darcie during my leave, I had wondered if I'd ever think about Camp Delta after I left, or if it would just recede into lost memory. I think about the camp often.

ACKNOWLEDGMENTS

The combined efforts of an amazing team made this book possible. All my thanks to my literary agent, Jeff Kleinman: He gave birth to this venture by responding to an e-mail from a concerned soldier who wanted to tell his story. Jeff offered outstanding guidance and always had my best interests at heart. My heartfelt appreciation goes to my coauthor, Viveca Novak, for the considerable skill with which she brought this story to life and her devotion to our shared mission. Also, special thanks to my publisher, Ann Godoff, and diligent editor, Emily Loose. Their decision to take a chance on this book, based on very little information, is one for which I'm forever grateful. I would also like to thank my attorney, Mark Zaid, who helped me navigate the legal intricacies of DOD's approval process.

So many others have helped shape this book through their actions—my parents, who taught me to have the courage to follow my convictions; my sisters, Wendy and Lori, who showed me the value of family; and my beautiful wife, Darcie, who has supported this idea from the outset and pushed me to do more than dream about this idea. She makes me a better man.

Last I'd like to thank all the men and women with whom I wore the uniform. Your daily sacrifices, both large and small, make us a much greater nation than most Americans even realize. You stand ready to make the ultimate sacrifice to defend freedom and our nation's values. The country owes you a debt of gratitude and I'm honored that I was allowed to stand next to you.

—E.S.

This book couldn't have happened without the support and encouragement of many people at *Time* magazine, especially Jim Kelly, Steve Koepp, and Michael Duffy; but also great friend and confidante Karen Tumulty, early booster Doug Waller, and all my other colleagues in the Washington bureau—the finest group of journalists I've ever had the great fortune to work with.

Thanks, too, to our agent, Jeff Kleinman, for his wisdom and advocacy. At Penguin Press, a thousand bouquets to our editor, Emily Loose, who lived this project with us and always provided just the right touch, and to Ann Godoff, who believed in this book from the beginning. Tracy Locke and Alex Lane were indispensable when the going got hot; they were always there for us. Thank you to Mahmoud Abdalla, director of Middlebury College's Language Schools, for backstopping our Arabic.

My deepest appreciation and admiration goes to Erik, who had the guts to realize that his story needed telling and set out to do it.

To Bob, Nora, and Thomas, all my love and endless gratitude for being the glue that kept me together, for making me smile, for your embrace, for looking to the future.

—V.N.

Appendix

Included in this appendix is the retyped text of the following selection of the U.S. government orders and memoranda pertaining to the treatment of detainees apprehended in the war on terror. The documents have been retyped for reading clarity. One original is provided here in a facsimile copy as well—the memo to Secretary of Defense Donald Rumsfeld from William J. Haynes II, General Counsel, Department of Defense, of November 27, 2002—with Donald Rumsfeld's handwritten notation. The originals of these documents as well as a number of additional government documents pertaining to the treatment of detainees and legal cases brought on behalf of terror suspects and detainees can be found at a number of Web sites. One site that is thorough and easy to navigate is that of the Project to Enforce the Geneva Conventions at http://pegc.no-ip.info. In addition, an extensive and authoritative compilation of the documents having to do with detainee treatment and legal standing is the book *The Torture Papers,* edited by Karen J. Greenberg and Joshua L. Dratel.

Due to their length, two important documents mentioned in the epilogue are not included here. One is the January 9, 2002 memorandum written by Deputy Assistant Attorney General John Yoo and Special Counsel Robert J. Delahunty to General Counsel William J. Haynes II, on the application of international treaties and laws, including the Geneva Convention, to the treatment of terrorist suspects apprehended in the conflict in Afghanistan. The other is the January 22, 2002 memorandum written by Assistant Attorney General Jay S. Bybee to Alberto R. Gonzales and William J. Haynes. They provide the government's legal arguments about why the Geneva Convention does not apply to suspected Al Qaeda and Taliban detainees.

1. Order issued by President Bush, November 13, 2001
    Re: Detention, Treatment, and Trial of Certain Non-Citizens in the War Against Terrorism
2. Memorandum to President Bush from Alberto R. Gonzales, Counsel to the President, January 25, 2002
    Re: Decision Re Application of the Geneva Convention on Prisoners of War to the Conflict with Al Qaeda and the Taliban
3. Memorandum to Alberto R. Gonzales from Secretary of State Colin Powell, January 26, 2002
    Re: Draft Decision Memorandum for the President on the Applicability of the Geneva Convention to the Conflict in Afghanistan

4. Text of order signed by President Bush on February 7, 2002, outlining treatment of al-Qaida and Taliban detainees

5. Action memo to Donald Rumsfeld, Secretary of Defense, from William J. Haynes II, General Counsel, Department of Defense, November 27, 2002
Re: Counter-Resistance Techniques

6. Department of Defense explanation of Guantánamo Interrogation Techniques, approved by Donald Rumsfeld, December 2002

7. Memorandum for Commander USSOUTHCOM from Donald Rumsfeld, January 15, 2003
Re: Counter-Resistance Techniques (U)

8. Memorandum for the Commander, US Southern Command from Donald Rumsfeld, April 16, 2003

President Issues Military Order
Detention, Treatment, and Trial of Certain Non-Citizens in the War Against Terrorism

By the authority vested in me as President and as Commander in Chief of the Armed Forces of the United States by the Constitution and the laws of the United States of America, including the Authorization for Use of Military Force Joint Resolution (Public Law 107-40, 115 Stat. 224) and sections 821 and 836 of title 10, United States Code, it is hereby ordered as follows:

Section 1. Findings.

(a) International terrorists, including members of al Qaida, have carried out attacks on United States diplomatic and military personnel and facilities abroad and on citizens and property within the United States on a scale that has created a state of armed conflict that requires the use of the United States Armed Forces.

(b) In light of grave acts of terrorism and threats of terrorism, including the terrorist attacks on September 11, 2001, on the headquarters of the United States Department of Defense in the national capital region, on the World Trade Center in New York, and on civilian aircraft such as in Pennsylvania, I proclaimed a national emergency on September 14, 2001 (Proc. 7463, Declaration of National Emergency by Reason of Certain Terrorist Attacks).

(c) Individuals acting alone and in concert involved in international terrorism possess both the capability and the intention to undertake further terrorist attacks against the United States that, if not detected and prevented, will cause mass deaths, mass injuries, and massive destruction of property, and may place at risk the continuity of the operations of the United States Government.

(d) The ability of the United States to protect the United States and its citizens, and to help its allies and other cooperating nations protect their nations and their citizens, from such further terrorist attacks depends in significant part upon using the United States Armed Forces to identify terrorists and those who support them, to disrupt their activities, and to eliminate their ability to conduct or support such attacks.

(e) To protect the United States and its citizens, and for the effective conduct of military operations and prevention of terrorist attacks, it is necessary for individuals subject to this order pursuant to section 2 hereof to be detained, and, when tried, to be tried for violations of the laws of war and other applicable laws by military tribunals.

(f) Given the danger to the safety of the United States and the nature of international terrorism, and to the extent provided by and under this order, I find consistent with section 836 of title 10, United States Code, that it is not practicable to apply in military commissions under this order the principles of law and the rules of evidence generally recognized in the trial of criminal cases in the United States district courts.

(g) Having fully considered the magnitude of the potential deaths, injuries, and property destruction that would result from potential acts of terrorism against the United States, and the probability that such acts will occur, I have determined that an extraordinary emergency exists for national defense purposes, that this emergency constitutes an urgent and compelling govern-ment interest, and that issuance of this order is necessary to meet the emergency.

Sec. 2. Definition and Policy.

(a) The term "individual subject to this order" shall mean any individual who is not a United States citizen with respect to whom I determine from time to time in writing that:

(1) there is reason to believe that such individual, at the relevant times,

(i) is or was a member of the organization known as al Qaida;

(ii) has engaged in, aided or abetted, or conspired to commit, acts of international terrorism, or acts in preparation therefor, that have caused, threaten to cause, or have as their aim to cause, injury to or adverse effects on the United States, its citizens, national security, foreign policy, or economy; or

(iii) has knowingly harbored one or more individuals described in subparagraphs (i) or (ii) of subsection 2(a)(1) of this order;

and

(2) it is in the interest of the United States that such individual be subject to this order.

(b) It is the policy of the United States that the Secretary of Defense shall take all necessary measures to ensure that any individual subject to this order is detained in accordance with section 3, and, if the individual is to be tried, that such individual is tried only in accordance with section 4.

(c) It is further the policy of the United States that any individual subject to this order who is not already under the control of the Secretary of Defense but who is under the control of any other officer or agent of the United States or any State shall, upon delivery of a copy of such written determination to such officer or agent, forthwith be placed under the control of the Secretary of Defense.

Sec. 3. Detention Authority of the Secretary of Defense. Any individual subject to this order shall be—

(a) detained at an appropriate location designated by the Secretary of Defense outside or within the United States;

(b) treated humanely, without any adverse distinction based on race, color, religion, gender, birth, wealth, or any similar criteria;

(c) afforded adequate food, drinking water, shelter, clothing, and medical treatment;

(d) allowed the free exercise of religion consistent with the requirements of such detention; and

(e) detained in accordance with such other conditions as the Secretary of Defense may prescribe.

Sec. 4. Authority of the Secretary of Defense Regarding Trials of Individuals Subject to this Order.

(a) Any individual subject to this order shall, when tried, be tried by military commission for any and all offenses triable by military commission that such individual is alleged to have committed, and may be punished in accordance with the penalties provided under applicable law, including life imprisonment or death.

(b) As a military function and in light of the findings in section 1, including subsection (f) thereof, the Secretary of Defense shall issue such orders and regulations, including orders for the appointment of one or more military commissions, as may be necessary to carry out subsection (a) of this section.

(c) Orders and regulations issued under subsection (b) of this section shall include, but not be limited to, rules for the conduct of the proceedings of military commissions, including pretrial, trial, and post-trial procedures, modes of proof, issuance of process, and qualifications of attorneys, which shall at a minimum provide for—

(1) military commissions to sit at any time and any place, consistent with such guidance regarding time and place as the Secretary of Defense may provide;

(2) a full and fair trial, with the military commission sitting as the triers of both fact and law;

(3) admission of such evidence as would, in the opinion of the presiding officer of the military commission (or instead, if any other member of the commission so requests at the time the presiding officer renders that opinion, the opinion of the commission rendered at that time by a majority of the commission), have probative value to a reasonable person;

(4) in a manner consistent with the protection of information classified or classifiable under Executive Order 12958 of April 17, 1995, as amended, or any successor Executive Order, protected by statute or rule from unauthorized disclosure, or otherwise protected by law, (A) the handling of, admission into evidence of, and access to materials and information, and (B) the conduct, closure of, and access to proceedings;

(5) conduct of the prosecution by one or more attorneys designated by the Secretary of Defense and conduct of the defense by attorneys for the individual subject to this order;

(6) conviction only upon the concurrence of two-thirds of the members of the commission present at the time of the vote, a majority being present;

(7) sentencing only upon the concurrence of two-thirds of the members of the commission present at the time of the vote, a majority being present; and

(8) submission of the record of the trial, including any conviction or sentence, for review and final decision by me or by the Secretary of Defense if so designated by me for that purpose.

Sec. 5. Obligation of Other Agencies to Assist the Secretary of Defense.

Departments, agencies, entities, and officers of the United States shall, to the maximum extent permitted by law, provide to the Secretary of Defense such assistance as he may request to implement this order.

Sec. 6. Additional Authorities of the Secretary of Defense.

(a) As a military function and in light of the findings in section 1, the Secretary of Defense shall issue such orders and regulations as may be necessary to carry out any of the provisions of this order.

(b) The Secretary of Defense may perform any of his functions or duties, and may exercise any of the powers provided to him under this order (other than under section 4(c)(8) hereof) in accordance with section 113(d) of title 10, United States Code.

Sec. 7. Relationship to Other Law and Forums.

(a) Nothing in this order shall be construed to—

(1) authorize the disclosure of state secrets to any person not otherwise authorized to have access to them;

(2) limit the authority of the President as Commander in Chief of the Armed Forces or the power of the President to grant reprieves and pardons; or

(3) limit the lawful authority of the Secretary of Defense, any military commander, or any other officer or agent of the United States or of

any State to detain or try any person who is not an individual subject to this order.

(b) With respect to any individual subject to this order—

(1) military tribunals shall have exclusive jurisdiction with respect to offenses by the individual; and

(2) the individual shall not be privileged to seek any remedy or maintain any proceeding, directly or indirectly, or to have any such remedy or proceeding sought on the individual's behalf, in (i) any court of the United States, or any State thereof, (ii) any court of any foreign nation, or (iii) any international tribunal.

(c) This order is not intended to and does not create any right, benefit, or privilege, substantive or procedural, enforceable at law or equity by any party, against the United States, its departments, agencies, or other entities, its officers or employees, or any other person.

(d) For purposes of this order, the term "State" includes any State, district, territory, or possession of the United States.

(e) I reserve the authority to direct the Secretary of Defense, at any time hereafter, to transfer to a governmental authority control of any individual subject to this order. Nothing in this order shall be construed to limit the authority of any such governmental authority to prosecute any individual for whom control is transferred.

Sec. 8. Publication.

This order shall be published in the Federal Register.

GEORGE W. BUSH
THE WHITE HOUSE,
November 13, 2001.

January 25, 2002

MEMORANDUM FOR THE PRESIDENT

FROM: ALBERTO R. GONZALES

SUBJECT: DECISION RE APPLICATION OF THE GENEVA CON-
VENTION ON PRISONERS OF WAR TO THE CON-
FLICT WITH AL QAEDA AND THE TALIBAN

Purpose

On January 18, I advised you that the Department of Justice had issued a formal legal opinion concluding that the Geneva Convention III
on the Treatment of Prisoners of War (GPW) does not apply to the
conflict with al Qaeda. I also advised you that DOJ's opinion concludes
that there are reasonable grounds for you to conclude that GPW does
not apply with respect to the conflict with the Taliban. I understand that
you decided that GPW does not apply and, accordingly, that al Qaeda
and Taliban detainees are not prisoners of war under the GPW.

The Secretary of State has requested that you reconsider that decision. Specifically, he has asked that you conclude that GPW does
apply to both al Qaeda and the Taliban. I understand, however, that
he would agree that al Qaeda and Taliban fighters could be determined not to be prisoners of war (POWs) but only on a case-by-case
basis following individual hearings before a military board.

This memorandum outlines the ramifications of your decision and
the Secretary's request for reconsideration.

Legal Background

As an initial matter, I note that you have the constitutional authority to make the determination you made on January 18 that the
GPW does not apply to al Qaeda and the Taliban. (Of course, you

could nevertheless, as a matter of policy, decide to apply the principles of GPW to the conflict with al Qaeda and the Taliban.) The Office of Legal Counsel of the Department of Justice has opined that, as a matter of international and domestic law, GPW does not apply to the conflict with al Qaeda. OLC has further opined that you have the authority to determine that GPW does not apply to the Taliban. As I discussed with you, the grounds for such a determination may include:

- A determination that Afghanistan was a failed state because the Taliban did not exercise full control over the territory and people, was not recognized by the international community, and was not capable of fulfilling its international obligations (e.g., was in widespread material breach of its international obligations).
- A determination that the Taliban and its forces were, in fact, not a government, but a militant, terrorist-like group.

OLC's interpretation of this legal issue is definitive. The Attorney General is charged by statute with interpreting the law for the Executive Branch. This interpretive authority extends to both domestic and international law. He has, in turn, delegated this role to OLC. Nevertheless, you should be aware that the Legal Adviser to the Secretary of State has expressed a different view.

Ramifications of Determination that GPW Does Not Apply

The consequences of a decision to adhere to what I understood to be your earlier determination that the GPW does not apply to the Taliban include the following:

Positive:

- Preserves flexibility:
  o As you have said, the war against terrorism is a new kind of war. It is not the traditional clash between nations adhering to the laws of war that formed the backdrop for GPW. The nature of the new war places a high premium on other factors, such as the ability to quickly obtain information from captured terrorists and their sponsors in order to avoid further atrocities against American

civilians, and the need to try terrorists for war crimes such as wantonly killing civilians. In my judgment, this new paradigm renders obsolete Geneva's strict limitations on questioning of enemy prisoners and renders quaint some of its provisions requiring that captured enemy be afforded such things as commissary privileges, scrip (i.e., advances of monthly pay), athletic uniforms, and scientific instruments.

- o Although some of these provisions do not apply to detainees who are not POWs, a determination that GPW does not apply to al Qaeda and the Taliban eliminates any argument regarding the need for case-by-case determinations of POW status. It also holds open options for the future conflicts in which it may be more difficult to determine whether an enemy force as a whole meets the standard for POW status.
- o By concluding that GPW does not apply to al Qaeda and the Taliban, we avoid foreclosing options for the future, particularly against nonstate actors.
- Substantially reduces the threat of domestic criminal prosecution under the War Crimes Act (18 U.S.C. 2441).
  - o That statute, enacted in 1996, prohibits the commission of a "war crime" by or against a U.S. person, including U.S. officials. "War crime" for these purposes is defined to include any grave breach of GPW or any violation of common Article 3 thereof (such as "outrages against personal dignity"). Some of these provisions apply (if the GPW applies) regardless of whether the individual being detained qualifies as a POW. Punishments for violations of Section 2441 include the death penalty. A determination that the GPW is not applicable to the Taliban would mean that Section 2441 would not apply to actions taken with respect to the Taliban.
  - o Adhering to your determination that GPW does not apply would guard effectively against misconstruction or misapplication of Section 2441 for several reasons.
  - o First, some of the language of the GPW is undefined (it prohibits, for example, "outrages upon personal dignity" and "inhuman treatment"), and it is difficult to predict with confidence what actions might be deemed to constitute violations of the relevant provisions of GPW.
  - o Second, it is difficult to predict the needs and circumstances that could arise in the course of the war on terrorism.

o Third, it is difficult to predict the motives of prosecutors and independent counsels who may in the future decide to pursue unwarranted charges based on Section 2441. Your determination would create a reasonable basis in law that Section 2441 does not apply, which would provide a solid defense to any future prosecution.

Negative:

On the other hand, the following arguments would support reconsideration and reversal of your decision that the GPW does not apply to either al Qaeda or the Taliban:

- Since the Geneva Conventions were concluded in 1949, the United States has never denied their applicability to either U.S. or opposing forces engaged in armed conflict, despite several opportunities to do so. During the last Bush Administration, the United States stated that it "has a policy of applying the Geneva Conventions of 1949 whenever armed hostilities occur with regular foreign armed forces, even if arguments could be made that the threshold standards for the applicability of the Conventions . . . are not met."
- The United States could not invoke the GPW if enemy forces threatened to mistreat or mistreated U.S. or coalition forces captured during operations in Afghanistan, or if they denied Red Cross access or other POW privileges.
- The War Crimes Act could not be used against the enemy, although other criminal statutes and the customary law of war would still be available.
- Our position would likely provoke widespread condemnation among our allies and in some domestic quarters, even if we make clear that we will comply with the core humanitarian principles of the treaty as a matter of policy.
- Concluding that the Geneva Convention does not apply may encourage other countries to look for technical "loopholes" in future conflicts to conclude that they are not bound by GPW either.
- Other countries may be less inclined to turn over terrorists or provide legal assistance to us if we do not recognize a legal obligation to comply with the GPW.
- A determination that GPW does not apply to al Qaeda and the Taliban could undermine U.S. military culture which emphasizes main-

taining the highest standards of conduct in combat, and could introduce an element of uncertainty in the status of adversaries.

Responses to Arguments for Applying GPW to the al Qaeda and the
Taliban

On balance, I believe that the arguments for reconsideration and
reversal are unpersuasive.

- The argument that the U.S. has never determined that GPW did not
  apply is incorrect. In at least one case (Panama in 1989) the U.S.
  determined that GPW did not apply even though it determined for
  policy reasons to adhere to the convention. More importantly, as
  noted above, this is a new type of warfare—one not contemplated in
  1949 when the GPW was framed—and requires a new approach in
  our actions toward captured terrorists. Indeed as the statement
  quoted from the administration of President George Bush makes
  clear, the U.S. will apply GPW "whenever hostilities occur *with regular armed forces.*" By its terms, therefore, the policy does not apply
  to a conflict with terrorists, or with irregular forces, like the Taliban,
  who are armed militants that oppressed and terrorized the people
  of Afghanistan.
- In response to the argument that we should decide to apply GPW to
  the Taliban in order to encourage other countries to treat captured
  U.S. military personnel in accordance with the GPW, it should be
  noted that your policy of providing human treatment to enemy detainees gives us the credibility to insist on like treatment for our soldiers. Moreover, even if GPW is not applicable, we can still bring
  war crimes charges against anyone who mistreats U.S. personnel.
  Finally, I note that our adversaries in several recent conflicts have
  not been deterred by GPW in their mistreatment of captured U.S.
  personnel, and terrorists will not follow GPW rules in any event.
- The statement that other nations would criticize the U.S. because
  we have determined that GPW does not apply is undoubtedly true.
  It is even possible that some nations would point to that determination as a basis for failing to cooperate with us on specific matters in
  the war against terrorism. On the other hand, some international
  and domestic criticism is already likely to flow from your previous
  decision not to treat the detainees as POWs. And we can facilitate

cooperation with other nations by reassuring them that we fully support GPW where it is applicable and by acknowledging that in this conflict the U.S. continues to respect other recognized standards.

- In the treatment of detainees, the U.S. will continue to be constrained by (i) its commitment to treat the detainees humanely and, to the extent appropriate and consistent with military necessity, in a manner consistent with the principles of GPW, (ii) its applicable treaty obligations, (iii) minimum standards of treatment universally recognized by the nations of the world, and (iv) applicable military regulations regarding the treatment of detainees.
- Similarly, the argument based on military culture fails to recognize that our military remain bound to apply the principals of GPW because that is what you have directed them to do.

United States Department of State

Washington, D.C. 20520

MEMORANDUM

TO: Counsel to the President

Assistant to the President for National Security Affairs

FROM: Colin L. Powell

SUBJECT: Draft Decision Memorandum for the President on the Applicability of the Geneva Convention to the Conflict in Afghanistan

I appreciate the opportunity to comment on the draft memorandum. I am concerned that the draft does not squarely present to the President the options that are available to him. Nor does it identify the significant pros and cons of each option. I hope that the final memorandum will make clear that the President's choice is between

Option 1: Determine that the Geneva Convention on the treatment of Prisoners of War (GPW) does not apply to the conflict on "failed State" or some other grounds. Announce this position publicly. Treat all detainees consistent with the principles of GPW;

and

Option 2: Determine that the Geneva Convention does apply to the conflict in Afghanistan, but that members of al Qaeda as a group and the Taliban individually or as a group are not entitled to Prisoner of War status under the Convention. Announce this position publicly. Treat all detainees consistent with the principles of the GPW.

The final memorandum should first tell the President that both options have the following advantages—that is there is no difference between them in these respects:

- Both provide the same practical flexibility in how we treat detainees, including with respect to interrogation and length of the detention.
- Both provide flexibility to provide conditions of detention and trial that take into account constraints such as feasibility under the circumstances and necessary security requirements.

- Both allow us not to give the privileges and benefits of POW status to al Qaeda and Taliban.
- Neither option entails and significant risk of domestic prosecution against U.S. officials.

The memorandum should go on to identify the separate pros and cons of the two options as follows:

Option 1—Geneva Convention does not apply to the conflict

Pros:

- This is an across-the-board approach that on its face provides maximum flexibility, removing any question of case-by-case determination for individuals.

Cons:

- It will reverse over a century of U.S. policy and practice in supporting the Geneva conventions and undermine the protections of the law of war for our troops, both in this specific conflict and in general.
- It has a high cost in terms of negative international reaction, with immediate adverse consequences for our conduct of foreign policy.
- It will undermine public support among critical allies, making military cooperation more difficult to sustain.
- Europeans and others will likely have legal problems with extradition or others forms of cooperation in law enforcement, including in bringing terrorists to justice.
- It may provoke some individual foreign prosecutors to investigate and prosecute our officials and troops.
- It will make us more vulnerable to domestic and international legal challenge and deprive us of important legal options:
  - It undermines the President's Military Order by removing an important legal basis for trying the detainees before Military Commissions.
  - We will be challenged in international fora (UN Commission on Human Rights; World Court; etc.).
  - The Geneva Conventions are a more flexible and suitable legal

framework than other laws that would arguably apply (customary international human rights, human rights conventions). The GPW permits long-term detention without criminal charges. Even after the President determines hostilities have ended, detention continues if criminal investigations or proceedings are in process. The GPW also provides clear authority for transfer of detainees to third countries.

– Determining GPW does not apply deprives us of a winning argument to oppose habeas corpus actions in U.S. Courts.

Option 2—Geneva Convention applies to the conflict

Pros:

• By providing a more defensible legal framework, it preserves our flexibility under both domestic and international law.
• It provides the strongest legal foundation for what we actually intend to do.
• It presents a positive international posture, preserves U.S. credibility and moral authority by taking the high ground, and puts us in a better position to demand and receive international support.
• It maintains POW status for U.S. forces, reinforces the importance of the Geneva Conventions, and generally supports the U.S. objective of ensuring its forces are accorded protection under the Convention.
• It reduces the incentive for international criminal investigations directed against U.S. officials and troops.

Cons:

• If, for some reason, a case-by-case review is used for Taliban, some may be determined to be entitled to POW status. This would not, however, affect their treatment as a practical matter.

I hope that you can restructure the memorandum along these lines, which it seems to me will give the President a much clearer understanding of the options available to him and their consequences. Quite aside from the need to identify options and their consequences more clearly, in its present form, the draft memorandum is inaccurate or incomplete in several respects. The most important factual errors are identified on the attachment.

Comments on the Memorandum of January 25, 2002

Purpose

(Second paragraph) The Secretary of State believes that al Qaeda terrorists as a group are not entitled to POW status and that Taliban fighters could be determined not to be POW's either as a group or on a case-by-case basis.

Legal Background

(First bullet) The Memorandum should note that any determination that Afghanistan is a failed state would be contrary to the official U.S. government position. The United States and the international community have consistently held Afghanistan to its treaty obligations and identified it as a party to the Geneva Conventions.

(Second paragraph) The Memorandum should note that the OLC interpretation does not preclude the President from reaching a different conclusion. It should also note that the OLC opinion is likely to be rejected by foreign governments and will not be respected in foreign courts or international tribunals which may assert jurisdiction over the subject matter. It should also note that OLC views are not definitive on the factual questions which are central to its legal conclusions.

Ramifications of Determination that GPW Does Not Apply

(Positive) The Memorandum identifies several positive consequences if the President determines the GPW does not apply. The Memorandum should note that these consequences would result equally if the President determines that the GPW does apply but that the detainees are not entitled to POW status.

(Negative. First bullet) The first sentence is correct as it stands. The second sentence is taken out of context and should be omitted.

The U.S. position in Panama was that Common Article 3 of the Geneva Conventions did apply.

Response to Arguments for Applying GPW to the al Qaeda and the Taliban

(First bullet) The assertion in the first sentence is incorrect. The United States has never determined that the GPW did not apply to an armed conflict in which its forces have been engaged. With respect to the third sentence, while no-one anticipated the precise situation that we face, the GPW was intended to cover all types of armed conflict and did not by its terms limit its application.

(Fourth bullet) The point is not clear. If we intend to conform our treatment of the detainees to universally recognized standards, we will be complying with the GPW.

UNCLASSIFIED

THE WHITE HOUSE

WASHINGTON

February 7, 2002

MEMORANDUM FOR   THE VICE PRESIDENT
THE SECRETARY OF STATE
THE SECRETARY OF DEFENSE
THE ATTORNEY GENERAL
CHIEF OF STAFF TO THE PRESIDENT
DIRECTOR OF CENTRAL
    INTELLIGENCE
ASSISTANT TO THE PRESIDENT FOR
    NATIONAL SECURITY AFFAIRS
CHAIRMAN OF THE JOINT CHIEFS OF
    STAFF

SUBJECT: Human Treatment of al Qaeda and Taliban
Detainees

1. Our recent extensive discussions regarding the status of al-Qaida
and Taliban detainees confirm that the application of Geneva
Convention Relative to the Treatment of Prisoners of War of August 12, 1949, (Geneva) to the conflict with al-Qaida and the Taliban involves complex legal questions. By its terms, Geneva
applies to conflicts involving "High Contracting Parties," which can
only be states. Moreover, it assumes the existence of "regular"
armed forces fighting on behalf of states. However, the war
against terrorism ushers in a new paradigm, one in which groups
with broad, international reach commit horrific acts against innocent civilians, sometimes with the direct support of states. Our nation recognizes that this new paradigm—ushered in not by us, but
by terrorists—requires new thinking in the law of war, but thinking
that should nevertheless be consistent with the principles of
Geneva.

2. Pursuant to my authority as commander in chief and chief executive of the United States, and relying on the opinion of the Department of Justice dated January 22, 2002, and on the legal opinion rendered by the attorney general in his letter of February 1, 2002, I hereby determine as follows:

    a. I accept the legal conclusion of the Department of Justice and determine that none of the provisions of Geneva apply to our conflict with al-Qaida in Afghanistan or elsewhere throughout the world because, among other reasons, al-Qaida is not a High Contracting Party to Geneva.

    b. I accept the legal conclusion of the attorney general and the Department of Justice that I have the authority under the Constitution to suspend Geneva as between the United States and Afghanistan, but I decline to exercise that authority at this time. Accordingly, I determine that the provisions of Geneva will apply to our present conflict with the Taliban. I reserve the right to exercise the authority in this or future conflicts.

    c. I also accept the legal conclusion of the Department of Justice and determine that common Article 3 of Geneva does not apply to either al-Qaida or Taliban detainees, because, among other reasons, the relevant conflicts are international in scope and common Article 3 applies only to "armed conflict not of an international character."

    d. Based on the facts supplied by the Department of Defense and the recommendation of the Department of Justice, I determine that the Taliban detainees are unlawful combatants and, therefore, do not qualify as prisoners of war under Article 4 of Geneva. I note that, because Geneva does not apply to our conflict with al-Qaida, al-Qaida detainees also do not qualify as prisoners of war.

3. Of course, our values as a nation, values that we share with many nations in the world, call for us to treat detainees humanely, including those who are not legally entitled to such treatment. Our nation has been and will continue to be a strong supporter of Geneva and its principles. As a matter of policy, the United States Armed Forces shall continue to treat detainees humanely and, to

the extent appropriate and consistent with military necessity, in a manner consistent with the principles of Geneva.

4. The United States will hold states, organizations, and individuals who gain control of United States personnel responsible for treating such personnel humanely and consistent with applicable law.

5. I hereby reaffirm the order previously issued by the secretary of defense to the United States Armed Forces requiring that the detainees be treated humanely and, to the extent appropriate and consistent with military necessity, in a manner consistent with the principles of Geneva.

6. I hereby direct the secretary of state to communicate my determinations in an appropriate manner to our allies, and other countries and international organizations cooperating in the war against terrorism of global reach.

GENERAL COUNSEL OF THE DEPARTMENT OF DEFENSE
1000 DEFENSE PENTAGON
WASHINGTON, D.C. 20301–1000

OFFICE OF THE SECRETARY OF DEFENSE
November 27, 2003 (1:00 PM)   DEPSEC_____
FOR: SECRETARY OF DEFENSE

FROM: William J. Haynes, II, General Counsel

SUBJECT: Counter-Resistance Techniques

- The Commander of USSOUTHCOM has forwarded a request by the Commander of Joint Task Force 170 (now JTF GTMO) for approval of counter-resistance techniques to aid in the interrogation of detainees at Guantanamo Bay (Tab A).
- The request contains three categories of counter-resistance techniques, with the first category the least aggressive and the third category the most aggressive (Tab B).
- I have discussed this with the Deputy, Doug Feith and General Myers. I believe that all join in my recommendation that, as a matter of policy, you authorize the Commander of USSOUTH-COM to empoloy, in his discretion, only Categories I and II and the fourth technique listed in Category III ("Use of mild, non-injurious physical contact such as grabbing, poking in the chest with the finger, and light pushing").
- While all Category III techniques may be legally available, we believe that, as a matter of policy, a blanket approval of Category III techniques is not warranted at this time. Our Armed Forces are trained to a standard of interrogation that reflects a tradition of restraint.

RECOMMENDATION: That SECDEF approve the USSOUTHCOM Commander's use of those counter-resistance techniques listed in Categories I and II and the fourth technique listed in Category III during the interrogation of detainees at Guantanamo Bay.

SECDEF DECISION:

Approved [signature of Donald Rumsfeld]
Disapproved———————
Other————————
Attachments
As stated   **Handwritten note:** However, I stand up for
                                   8-10 hours a day. Why is standing limited to
                                   4 hours? D.R.

cc: CJCS, USD (P)
Declassified under Authority of Executive Order 12958
By Executive Secretary, Office of the Secretary of Defense
William P. Marrion, CAPT. USN
June 18, 2004

− C.
− I.D.

GENERAL COUNSEL OF THE DEPARTMENT OF DEFENSE
1600 DEFENSE PENTAGON
WASHINGTON, D.C. 20301-1600

2002 DEC -2 AM 11: 03

GENERAL COUNSEL

OFFICE OF THE
SECRETARY OF DEFENSE

ACTION MEMO

November 27, 2002 (1:00 PM)

DEPSEC_____

FOR: SECRETARY OF DEFENSE

FROM: William J. Haynes II, General Counsel

SUBJECT: Counter-Resistance Techniques

- The Commander of USSOUTHCOM has forwarded a request by the Commander of Joint Task Force 170 (now JTF GTMO) for approval of counter-resistance techniques to aid in the interrogation of detainees at Guantanamo Bay (Tab A).

- The request contains three categories of counter-resistance techniques, with the first category the least aggressive and the third category the most aggressive (Tab B).

- I have discussed this with the Deputy, Doug Feith and General Myers. I believe that all join in my recommendation that, as a matter of policy, you authorize the Commander of USSOUTHCOM to employ, in his discretion, only Categories I and II and the fourth technique listed in Category III ("Use of mild, non-injurious physical contact such as grabbing, poking in the chest with the finger, and light pushing").

- While all Category III techniques may be legally available, we believe that, as a matter of policy, a blanket approval of Category III techniques is not warranted at this time. Our Armed Forces are trained to a standard of interrogation that reflects a tradition of restraint.

RECOMMENDATION: That SECDEF approve the USSOUTHCOM Commander's use of those counter-resistance techniques listed in Categories I and II and the fourth technique listed in Category III during the interrogation of detainees at Guantanamo Bay.

SECDEF DECISION

Approved _____ Disapproved _____ Other _____

Attachments
As stated

cc: CJCS, USD(P)

However, I stand for 8-10 hours a day. Why is standing limited to 4 hours?

D.R. DEC 0 2 2002

Page 2 of
X C4C30

Department of Defense
Category I, II, and III Interrogation Techniques

Approved by Secretary of Defense in December 2002

Used December 2002 through 15 January 2003

Category I

- Incentive
- Yelling at Detainee
- Deception
- Multiple Interrogator techniques
- Interrogator identity

Category II

- Stress positions for a maximum of four hours (e.g., standing)
- Use of falsified documents or reports
- Isolation up to 30 days (requires notice)
- Interrogation outside of the standard interrogation booth
- Deprivation of light and auditory stimuli
- Hooding during transport & interrogation
- Use of 20-hour interrogations
- Removal of all comfort items
- Switching detainee from hot meal to MRE
- Removal of clothing
- Forced grooming (e.g., shaving)
- Inducing stress by use of detainee's fears (e.g., dogs)

Category III

- Use of mild, non-injurious physical contact

Category I

- Yelling (Not directly into ear)
- Deception (Introducing of confederate detainee)
- Role-playing interrogator in next cell

Category II

- Removal from social support at Camp Delta
- Segregation in Navy Brig
- Isolation in Camp X-ray
- Interrogating the detainee in an environment other than standard interrogation room at Camp Delta (i.e., Camp X-ray)
- Deprivation of light (use of red light)
- Inducing stress (use of female interrogator)
- Up to 20-hour interrogations
- Removal of all comfort items, including religious items
- Serving MRE instead of hot rations
- Forced grooming (to include shaving facial hair and head— also served hygienic purposes)
- Use of false documents or reports

THE SECRETARY OF DEFENSE
1000 DEFENSE PENTAGON
WASHINGTON, D.C. 20301-1000

MEMORANDUM FOR COMMANDER USSOUTHCOM

JAN 15 2003

SUBJECT: Counter-Resistance Techniques (U)

(S) My December 2, 2002, approval of the use of all Category II techniques and one Category III technique during interrogations at Guantanamo is hereby rescinded. Should you determine that particular techniques in either of these categories are warranted in an individual case, you should forward that request to me. Such a request should include a thorough justification for the employment of those techniques and a detailed plan for the use of such techniques.

(U) In all interrogations, you should continue the humane treatment of detainees, regardless of the type of interrogation technique employed.

(U) Attached is a memo to the General Counsel setting in motion a study to be completed within 15 days. After my review, I will provide further guidance.

THE SECRETARY OF DEFENSE
1000 DEFENSE PENTAGON
WASHINGTON, D.C. 20301-1000

APRIL 16 2003

MEMORANDUM FOR THE COMMANDER, US SOUTHERN COMMAND

SUBJECT: Counter-Resistance Techniques in the War on Terrorism (S)

~~(S/NF)~~ (U) I have considered the report of the Working Group that I directed be established on January 15, 2003.

~~(S/NF)~~ (U) I approve the use of specified counter-resistance techniques, subject to the following:

(U) a. The techniques I authorize are those lettered A-X, set out at Tab A.

(U) b. These techniques must be used with all the safeguards described at Tab B.

~~(S)~~ (U) c. Use of these techniques is limited to interrogations of unlawful combatants held at Guantanamo Bay, Cuba.

~~(S)~~ (U) d. Prior to the use of these techniques, the Chairman of the Working Group on Detainee Interrogations in the Global War on Terrorism must brief you and your staff.

~~(S/NF)~~ (U) I reiterate that US Armed Forces shall continue to treat detainees humanely, and, to the extent appropriate and consistent with military necessity, in a manner consistent with the principles of the Geneva Conventions. In addition, if you intend to use techniques B, I, O, or X, you must specifically determine that military necessity requires its use and notify me in advance.

(~~(S/NF)~~ U) If, in your view, you require additional interrogation techniques for a particular detainee, you should provide me, via the Chairman of the Joint Chiefs of Staff, a written request describing the proposed technique, recommended safeguards, and the rationale for applying it with an identified detainee.

~~(S/NF)~~ (U) Nothing in this memorandum in any way restricts your existing authority to maintain good order and discipline among detainees.

Attachments:	Classified by: Secretary of
As stated	Defense
	Reason: 1.5(a)
	Declassify On: 2 April 2013

TAB A

INTERROGATION TECHNIQUES

(S/NF) (U) The use of techniques A-X is subject to the general safe-guards as provided below as well as specific implementation guide-lines to be provided by the appropriate authority. Specific implementation guidance with respect to techniques A-Q is provided in Army Field Manual 34–52. Further implementation guidance with respect to techniques R-X will need to be developed by the appropriate authority.

(S/NF) (U) Of the techniques set forth below, the policy aspects of certain techniques should be considered to the extent those policy aspects reflect the views of other major U.S. partner nations. Where applicable, the description of the technique is annotated to include a summary of the policy issues that should be considered before application of the technique.

A. (S/NF) (U) Direct: Asking straightforward questions.

B. (S/NF) (U) Incentive/Removal of Incentive: Providing a reward or removing a privilege, above and beyond those that are required by the Geneva Convention, from detainees. [Caution: Other nations that believe that detainees are entitled to POW protections may consider that provsision and retention of religious items (e.g., the Koran) are protected under international law (see, Geneva III, Article 34). Al-though the provisions of the Geneva Convention are not applicable to the interrogation of unlawful combatants, consideration should be given to these views prior to application of the techniques.]

C. (S/NF) (U) Emotional Love: Playing on the love a detainee has for an individual or group.

D. (S/NF) (U) Emotional Hate: Playing on the hatred a detainee has for an individual or group.

E. ~~(S/NF)~~ (U) Fear Up Harsh: Significantly increasing the fear level in a detainee.

F. ~~(S/NF)~~ (U) Fear Up Mild: Moderately increasing the fear level in a detainee.

G. ~~(S/NF)~~ (U) Reduced Fear: Reducing the fear level in a detainee.

H. ~~(S/NF)~~ (U) Pride and Ego Up: Boosting the ego of a detainee.

Classified By:	Secretary of Defense
Reason:	1.5(a)
Declassify On:	2 April 2013

NOT RELEASABLE TO
FOREIGN NATIONALS

UNCLASSIFIED

I. (S/NF) (U) Pride and Ego Down: Attacking or insulting the ego of a detainee, not beyond the limits that would apply to a POW. [Caution: Article 17 of Geneva III provides, "Prisoners of war who refuse to answer may not be threatened, insulted, or exposed to any unpleasant or disadvantageous treatment of any kind." Other nations that believe that detainees are entitled to POW protections may consider this technique inconsistent with the provisions of Geneva. Although the provisions of Geneva are not applicable to the interrogation of unlawful combatants, consideration should be given to these views prior to application of the technique.]

J. (S/NF) (U) Futility: Invoking the feeling of futility of a detainee.

K. (S/NF) (U) We Know All: Convincing the detainee that the interrogator knows the answer to questions he asks the detainee.

L. (S/NF) (U) Establish Your Identity: Convincing the detainee that the interrogator has mistaken the detainee for someone else.

M. (S/NF) (U) Repetition Approach: Continuously repeating the same question to the detainee within interrogation periods of normal duration.

N. (S/NF) (U) File and Dossier: Convincing detainee that the interrogator has a damning and inaccurate file, which must be fixed.

O. (S/NF) (U) Mutt and Jeff: A team consisting of a friendly and harsh interrogator. The harsh interrogator might employ the Pride and Ego Down technique. [Caution: Other nations that believe that POW protections apply to detainees may view this technique as inconsistent with Geneva III, Article 13 which provides that POWs must be protected against acts of intimidation. Although the provisions of Geneva are not applicable to the interrogation of unlawful combatants, consideration should be given to these views prior to application of the technique.]

P. (S/NF) (U) Rapid Fire: Questioning in rapid succession without allowing detainee to answer.

Q. (S/NF) (U) Silence: Staring at the detainee to encourage discomfort.

R. (S/NF) (U) Change of Scenery Up: Removing the detainee from the standard interrogation setting (generally to a location more pleasant, but no worse).

S. (S/NF) (U) Change of Scenery Down: Removing the detainee from the standard interrogation setting and placing him in a setting that may be less comfortable; would not constitute a substantial change in environmental quality.

T. (S/NF) (U) Dietary Manipulation: Changing the diet of a detainee; no intended deprivation of food or water; no adverse medical or cultural effect and without intent to deprive subject of food or water, e.g., hot rations to MREs.

U. (S/NF) (U) Environmental Manipulation: Altering the environment to create moderate discomfort (e.g., adjusting temperature or introducing an unpleasant smell). Conditions would not be such that they would injure the detainee. Detainee would be accompanied by interrogator at all times. [Caution: Based on court cases in other countries, some nations may view application of this technique in certain circumstances to be inhumane. Consideration of these views should be given prior to use of this technique.]

V. (S/NF) (U) Sleep Adjustment: Adjusting the sleeping times of the detainee (e.g., reversing sleep cycles from night to day.) This technique is NOT sleep deprivation.

W. (S/NF) (U) False Flag: Convincing the detainee that individuals from a country other than the United States are interrogating him.

X. (S/NF) (U) Isolation: Isolating the detainee from other detainees while still complying with basic standards of treatment. [Caution: The use of isolation as an interrogation technique requires detailed implementation instructions, including specific guidelines regarding the length of isolation, medical and psychological review, and approval for extensions of the length of isolation by the appropriate level in the chain of command. This technique is not known to have been generally used for interrogation purposes for longer than 30 days. Those nations that believe detainees are subject to POW protections may view use of this technique as inconsistent with the requirements of Geneva III, Article 13 which provides that POWs must be protected against acts of intimidation; Article 14 which provides that POWs are entitled to respect for their person; Article 34 which prohibits coercion and Article 126 which ensures access and basic standards of treatment. Although the provisions of Geneva are not applicable to the interrogation of unlawful combatants, consideration should be given to these views prior to application of the technique.]

UNCLASSIFIED

TAB B

GENERAL SAFEGUARDS

(S/NF) (U) Application of these interrogations techniques is subject to the following general safeguards: (i) limited to use only at strategic interrogation facilities; (ii) there is a good basis to believe that the detainee possesses critical intelligence; (iii) the detainee is medically and operationally evaluated as suitable (considering all techniques to be used in combination); (iv) interrogators are specifically trained for the technique(s); (v) a specific interrogation plan (including reasonable safeguards, limits on duration, intervals between applications, termination criteria and the presence or availability of qualified medical personnel) has been developed; (vi) there is appropriate supervision; and, (vii) there is appropriate specified senior approval for use with any specific detainee (after considering the foregoing and receiving legal advice).

(U) The purpose of all interviews and interrogations is to get the most information from a detainee with the least intrusive method, always applied in a humane and lawful manner with sufficient oversight by trained investigators or interrogators. Operating instructions must be developed based on command policies to insure uniform, careful, and safe application of any interrogations of detainees.

(S/NF) (U) Interrogations must always be planned, deliberate actions that take into account numerous, often interlocking factors such as a detainee's current and past performance in both detention and interrogation, a detainee's emotional and physical strengths and weaknesses, an assessment of possible approaches that may work on a certain detainee in an effort to gain the trust of the detainee, strengths and weaknesses of interrogators, and augmentation by other personnel for a certain detainee based on other factors.

(S/NF) (U) Interrogation approaches are designed to manipulate the detainee's emotions and weaknesses to gain his willing cooperation. Interrogation operations are never conducted in a vacuum; they are conducted in close cooperation with the units detaining the individuals. The policies established by the detaining units that pertain to searching, silencing, and segregating also play a role in the interrogation of a detainee. Detainee interrogation involves developing a plan tailored to an individual and approved by senior interrogators. Strict adherence to policies/standard operating procedures governing the administration of interrogation techniques and oversight is essential.

Classified By:	Secretary of Defense
Reason:	1.5(a)
Declassify On:	2 April 2013

(S/NF) (U) It is important that interrogators be provided reasonable latitude to vary techniques depending on the detainee's culture, strengths, weaknesses, environment, extent of training in resistance techniques as well as the urgency of obtaining information that the detainee is known to have.

(S/NF) (U) While techniques are considered individually within this analysis, it must be understood that in practice, techniques are usually used in combination; the cumulative effect of all techniques to be employed must be considered before any decisions are made regarding approval for particular situations. The title of a particular technique is not always fully descriptive of a particular technique. With respect to the employment of any techniques involving physical contact, stress or that could produce physical pain or harm, a detailed explanation of that technique must be provided to the decision authority prior to any decision.

ABOUT THE AUTHORS

Erik R. Saar served as an army sergeant with the U.S. military in the Detainee Camp at Guantánamo Bay, Cuba, for six months, from December 2002 to June 2003, working to support the intelligence and interrogation operations. Sergeant Saar is a recipient of two Good Conduct medals, an Army Commendation Medal, a Joint Service Commendation Medal, and a Joint Service Achievement Medal. He was trained in Arabic at the Defense Language Institute in Monterey, California. Before serving at Gitmo, he worked as an intelligence analyst for the National Security Agency at Fort Meade, Maryland, and for the FBI in New York City. He is a graduate of King's College in Wilkes-Barre, Pennsylvania.

Viveca Novak is a Washington correspondent for *Time*, covering legal affairs, terrorism, and civil liberties, among other issues. A recipient of Harvard University's Goldsmith Prize for investigative reporting, the Clarion Award for investigative reporting, and the Investigative Reporters and Editors Award, she is a frequent guest on the national broadcast media, including CNN, NBC, PBS, Fox, and MSNBC. She has a B.A. in foreign affairs from the University of Virginia, an M.S. from Columbia University School of Journalism, and an M.S.L. from Yale Law School.